Making Families Through Adoption

Contemporary Family Perspectives

A Series by Pine Forge Press, an imprint of SAGE Publications, Inc

Series Editor
Susan J. Ferguson
Grinnell College

Volumes in This Series

Families: A Social Class Perspective
Shirley A. Hill

Making Families Through Adoption
Nancy E. Riley and Krista E. Van Vleet

Forthcoming

Families and Health, Second Edition
Janet Grochowski

Global Families, Second Edition
Meg W. Karraker

Key Issues in American Family Policy
Janet Z. Giele

Family Caregiving in Later Life
Twyla Hill

Making Families Through Adoption

CONTEMPORARY
FAMILY
PERSPECTIVES

NANCY E. RILEY

Bowdoin College

KRISTA E. VAN VLEET

Bowdoin College

SUSAN J. FERGUSON, SERIES EDITOR

 |

PINE
FORGE

Los Angeles | London | New Delhi
Singapore | Washington DC

Los Angeles | London | New Delhi
Singapore | Washington DC

FOR INFORMATION:

Pine Forge Press
An Imprint of SAGE Publications, Inc.
2455 Teller Road
Thousand Oaks, California 91320
E-mail: order@sagepub.com

SAGE Publications Ltd.
1 Oliver's Yard
55 City Road
London EC1Y 1SP
United Kingdom

SAGE Publications India Pvt. Ltd.
B 1/I 1 Mohan Cooperative Industrial Area
Mathura Road, New Delhi 110 044
India

SAGE Publications Asia-Pacific Pte. Ltd.
33 Pekin Street #02-01
Far East Square
Singapore 048763

Acquisitions Editor: David Repetto
Editorial Assistant: Maggie Stanley
Production Editor: Kelle Schillaci
Copy Editor: Barbara Corrigan
Typesetter: C&M Digitals (P) Ltd.
Proofreader: Joyce Li
Indexer: Will Ragsdale
Cover Designer: Janet Kiesel
Marketing Manager: Erica DeLuca
Permissions Editor: Karen Ehrmann

Printed in the United States of America

Library of Congress Cataloging-in-Publication Data

Riley, Nancy.

Making families through adoption /
Nancy E. Riley, Krista E. Van Vleet.

p. cm. — (Contemporary family perspectives)
Includes bibliographical references and index.

ISBN 978-1-4129-9800-0 (pbk. : acid-free paper)

1. Adoption—United States. 2. Families—United States. 3. Intercountry adoption.
4. Interracial adoption. 5. Interethnic adoption.
6. Adoption. I. Van Vleet, Krista E., 1965- II. Title.

HV875.55.R55 2012
362.7340973—dc22   2011001743

This book is printed on acid-free paper.

11 12 13 14 15 10 9 8 7 6 5 4 3 2 1

Contents

Series Preface: Contemporary Family Perspectives   vii

Acknowledgments   xi

Introduction   1
    Making Families: The Inequalities and Intimacies of Adoption   1
    Adoption in the United States   9
       Definitions   9
       Adoption and Statistics   11

1. **Adoption Across Cultures**   15
    Ethnographic Cases   16
       The Preference for Fostering in West Africa   16
       The Commonality of Child Circulation in the Andes   21
       The Stigma of Adoption in the Middle East   24
    Exploring the Significance of Cases   26
       Debunking the Opposition between
          Natural and Adoptive Parents   27
       Who Is Responsible for Raising Children?   30
       History Comes Up Behind Us: Fostering and
          Adoption as Shaped by Context   31
    Conclusions   35

2. **Adoption in the United States: Historical Perspectives**   37
    Children's Role in Society   38
    What Makes a Family? Contradictions and
       Controversies in American Adoption   42
    The Growing Demand for Adoptable Babies and the Increased
       Regulation of Adoption: Who Are the Best Mothers?   44
    Adoption Secrecy in the Formation of As-If Families   46
    Making Families Through Adoption in the Postwar Period   48
    Adoption in the United States Today   50
       Open Adoption   52
    Conclusions   53

3. Adoption: Private Decisions, Public Influences   55
    Who Adopts? Who Is Adopted?   57
       Socioeconomic Class: The Power of Money   57
       The Children: Characteristics of Adopted Children   61
       The Parents: Marital Status and Sexual Orientation   62
    What Makes a Proper Family? Interpreting Social Norms   63
    The Role of the State   65
    Comparative Perspectives on Government's Role in Adoption   69
       Adoption in China   69
       Adoption in Norway   71
    Conclusions   72

4. Race, Ethnicity, and Racism in Adoption and Fosterage Systems   73
    Race: A Social Construct, a Forceful Reality   74
    Race in U.S. Adoption History   77
    Transracial Adoption: Issues and Debates   79
    The Foster System and Adoption in the United States   83
    Native Americans and Adoption in the
       United States and Canada   87
    Conclusions   91

5. The Practices of Transnational Adoption   94
    The Global Transfer of Children   96
    Rules Governing Intercountry Adoptions   99
    The Receiving Countries   101
       Early International Adoption as Humanitarian Aid   101
       The United States   104
       Adoption in Norway   105
    The Sending Countries   107
       Korea   107
       Romania   109
       Guatemala   111
       China and Its Abandoned Girls   113
    After Adoption: The Making of Transnational Families   116
    Conclusions   122

Conclusion   123

Bibliography   132

Further Exploration   143

Index   148

About the Authors   155

Series Preface

Contemporary Family Perspectives

Susan J. Ferguson

Grinnell College

The family is one of the most private and pervasive social institutions in U.S. society. At the same time, public discussions and debates about the institution of the family persist. Some scholars and public figures claim that the family is declining or dying or that the contemporary family is in crisis or is morally deficient. Other scholars argue that the family has been caught in the larger culture wars taking place in the United States. The current debates about legalizing same-sex marriage are one example of this larger public discussion about the institution of the family. Regardless of one's perspective—viewing the family as declining or caught in broader political struggles—scholars agree that the institution has undergone dramatic transformations in recent decades. U.S. demographic data reveal that fewer people are married, divorce rates remain high, at almost 50 percent, and more families are living in poverty. In addition, people are creating new kinds of families via Internet dating, cohabitation, single-parent adoption, committed couples living apart, donor insemination, and polyamorous relationships. The demographic data and ethnographic research on new family forms require that family scholars pay attention to a variety of family structures, processes, ideologies, and social norms. In particular, scholars need to address important questions about the family, such as, What is the future of marriage? Is divorce harmful to individuals, to the institution of the family, and/or to society? Why are rates of family violence so high? Are we living in a postdating culture? How do poverty and welfare policies affect families? How is child rearing changing now that so many parents work outside the home and children spend time with caretakers other than their parents? Finally, how are families socially constructed in various societies and cultures?

Most sociologists and family scholars agree that the family is a dynamic social institution that is continually changing as other social structures and individuals in society change. The family also is a social construction with complex and shifting age, gender, race, and social class meanings. Many excellent studies are currently investigating the changing structures of the institution of the family and the lived experiences and meanings of families. *Contemporary Family Perspectives* is a series of short texts and research monographs that provides a forum for the best of this burgeoning scholarship. The series aims to recognize the diversity of families that exist in the United States and globally. A second goal is for the series to better inform pedagogy and future family scholarship about this diversity of families. The series also seeks to connect family scholarship to a broader audience beyond the classroom by informing the public and by ensuring that family studies remain central to contemporary policy debates and to social action. Each short text contains the most outstanding current scholarship on the family from a variety of disciplines, including sociology, demography, policy studies, social work, human development, and psychology. Moreover, each short text is authored by a leading family scholar or scholars who bring their unique disciplinary perspective to an understanding of contemporary families.

Contemporary Family Perspectives provides the most advanced scholarship and up-to-date findings on the family. Each volume contains a brief overview of significant scholarship on that family topic, including critical current debates or areas of scholarly disagreement. In addition to providing an assessment of the latest findings related to their family topic, authors examine the family utilizing an intersectional framework of race-ethnicity, social class, gender, and sexuality. Much of the research is interdisciplinary, with a number of theoretical frameworks and methodological approaches presented. Several of the family scholars use a historical lens as well to ground their contemporary research. A particular strength of the series is that the short texts appeal to undergraduate students as well as to family scholars, but they are written in a way that makes them accessible to a larger public.

About This Volume

Making Families Through Adoption examines a critical family formation process—adoption. Currently, only 2.4 percent of U.S. families are formed through adoption. Historically and cross-culturally, however, the circulation of children through adoption or fostering has been a common practice. The authors, sociologist Nancy E. Riley and anthropologist Krista E. Van Vleet of Bowdoin College, argue that the current discourse on adoption is all about choice but that in reality, adoption is immersed in cultural and social beliefs, economic transactions, and political realities. Their research reveals that while adoption has distinctive qualities across certain cultures, social inequality is at the root of most adoptions: Women of lower statuses often give children to women and families of higher social statuses.

This book, *Making Families Through Adoption,* provides a comprehensive look at adoption in the United States and in other cultures. Riley and Van Vleet begin their analysis with working definitions of *adoption, fostering,* and *child circulation.* They then examine child circulation practices in other cultures to see how these practices are windows into the larger society. Adoption reveals broader social and cultural norms, including the meaning and attributes of family. Next, Riley and Van Vleet examine adoption in the United States using a historical lens.

They are particularly interested in U.S. historical constructions of what constitutes family and how the value and roles of children have changed over time. After laying this cross-cultural and historical groundwork, Riley and Van Vleet focus on adoption in the contemporary context. The next three chapters investigate U.S. adoption practices in depth by first looking at the influence of socioeconomic status, marital status, and sexual orientation of potential parents on adoption. They also examine how the characteristics of children and governmental policies influence these seemingly private decisions to adopt. The authors then explore race, ethnicity, and racism in adoption and fosterage systems in the United States before turning their attention to transnational adoption.

Making Families Through Adoption is relevant to courses on the family, social inequality, cross-cultural studies, and public policy. This book is a valuable resource to teachers and students in beginning to advanced courses in sociology, anthropology, women's studies, social work, policy studies, and family studies. It also finds an audience among individuals who may work with families, adoption, and foster care, such as social workers, counselors, and other human service providers.

Acknowledgments

Although each of us has been doing research on issues related to family and kinship for many years, the impetus for coauthoring a book about adoption grew out of our conversations with each other about teaching, research, and everyday life. We are very grateful to a group of colleagues with whom we have shared many challenging and exciting discussions about the literary and social-scientific representations of motherhood and family: Susan Bell, Sara Dickey, Elaine Hansen, Emily Kane, and Mary Beth Mills. Thanks to Susan Ferguson for her editorial insight and her efforts to pull together an excellent and timely series. We would like to express our appreciation for David Repetto, Astrid Virding, Kelle Schillaci, Maggie Stanley, and Barbara Corrigan; their efforts have made this a better book and working with Sage, a pleasure. We thank Bob Gardner for his help on the tables and figures throughout the book. Nancy Grant assisted us with producing the maps. Thanks to singer-songwriter Mary Gauthier, manager Mark Spector, and artist Lilli Carre for use of the CD image, "The Foundling." We are grateful to the following institutions for their generous financial support: Fulbright Hays, Wenner-Gren Foundation for Anthropological Research, Bowdoin College, and the Andrew W. Mellon Foundation. An initial analysis of Van Vleet's ethnographic work on relatedness in the Bolivian Andes has been published in *Performing Kinship: Narrative, Gender, and the Intimacies of Power in the Andes* (Van Vleet 2008).

For
Huamei, Sarah, and Fern
Isabel and Sophia

Introduction

Making Families: The Inequalities and Intimacies of Adoption

The very first picture of myself is when I was Korean. Not Korean American, not Korean adopted, just plain Korean. I sit, in white pajamas, on a woman's lap. She has no identity. Her face is not there, only a chin and wisps of short hair stare down at me. It is strange to think that my first exposure to language was Korean, that I sat on her lap listening to her talk to me in smooth flowing tongue. To this day, I love listening to Korean people speak with one another. I eavesdrop, closing my eyes and pretending I understand every word and am home.

—Beth Kyong Lo, a Korean adoptee
(Trenka, Oparah, and Shin 2006:167)

My father had said, "Don't look at the baby." But I went to the nursery and I said, "Which one is mine?" He was in the back and he was crying, screaming. . . . I had the biggest urge to run into that nursery and pick him up. But my father told me not to hold the baby, not to look at the baby, because it never happened. It never happened. I didn't have a baby.

—Sheryl, a birth mother who
relinquished her baby (Fessler 2007:177)

It's just my feeling about it, but if we had adopted a Caucasian child, I wouldn't have as much a need to find out what their heritage was. . . . We wouldn't have to go to Norwegian festivals

1

*if the kid happened to be Norwegian. But being Chinese is
different. . . . Having that connection to where they're from is
very important, because you can't fit in and get by as a nice
Jewish girl when you look like you're from China, and you are
from China.*

—John Levison, an adoptive
father of a Chinese girl (Dorow 2006b:234)

A doption has emerged from the silence of previous generations. Not only
books and news articles, but also Internet blogs and chats, talk shows
and everyday conversations, popular music and art, and legislation and public
policy reflect a politics of visibility and a growing normalcy of making families
through adoption (as an example, see Figure I.1). Although the views of those
involved in the process—whether intimately or peripherally—are not homoge-
neous, a rhetorics of choice pervades discourses on adoption in the contemporary United States. To give up or to take in a child; to foster or adopt in the
United States or to adopt internationally; to search for a birth parent or one's
national and ethnic roots or to emphasize one's belonging to this family, this
nation; to answer a stranger's query or to ignore it are only some of the choices
that those involved in adoption make.

Yet the notion that adoption is about choice also obscures the ways in
which adoption is tied to pervasive understandings of the naturalness of only
certain kinds of families and to long-lasting social and political economic
hierarchies that shape everyday life. Rickie Solinger (2001:22) has said that
"child transfer . . . almost always depends on extremely poor and/or culturally oppressed mothers who utterly lack choices." In the quotations with
which we begin this book, Beth, Sheryl, and John point to some of the
silences around adoption that have shaped the experiences of many people
in the United States and in societies throughout the world. Their words illuminate the personal, and sometimes intimate, quality of those experiences
and at the same time challenge us to consider the ways in which people's
choices, and their own gains and losses, are configured by broader social,
political, and economic relationships.

Understanding families in the twenty-first century requires us to give
attention to a variety of family forms and ideologies, processes, and norms.
Understanding adoption, more specifically, challenges us to acknowledge
the articulation of cultural and social beliefs, political transformations, and
economic transactions as they emerge in the experiences of individuals and
the relationships within and between states. In this book we recognize that

Figure I.1 Mary Gauthier, a singer-songwriter based in Nashville, released an album in 2010, *The Foundling;* it tells Mary's story of being abandoned at an orphanage in New Orleans in 1962 and her later search for her birth parents

Source: Illustration by Mary Gauthier

fostering and adoption, and various other forms of "child circulation" (Fonseca 1986:15) in which the responsibility for the care and nurturance of a child is transferred from one adult to another, have developed in different societies and historical moments. Understanding the complexity of these relationships is significant for how we understand adoption itself, families more generally, and the social and political and economic inequalities that structure those realities in the United States.

As sociologist Barbara Katz Rothman (2005:27-28) has noted, the job of a social scientist is

> to make simple things complicated . . . to take something that looked pretty straightforward, pretty obvious, and show just how nonobvious it was, how many things went into creating the obvious reality before us. . . . We unravel the strands, look for hidden structures, see how things are constructed, how they are put together to seem so obvious.

Adoption, the movement of children from one family to another, is well served by this kind of perspective, one that social scientists call the "sociological imagination" (Mills 1959). Adoption may seem straightforward: One or more adults permanently or temporarily relinquish part or all of their rights and responsibilities for a child while one or more adults take on those rights and responsibilities. But the movement of a child from one place to another—from one household to another, one community to another, one country to another—is often very complicated. To some extent, the transfer of a child necessarily depends on shared agreement and acceptance of such a transfer. Adults, however, take part in the transaction for many reasons and under varying circumstances; the child may have little or no voice in the matter. The channels through which children pass and the direction of children's movements are often shaped by prevailing power relationships no matter what the personal intentions or emotional engagement of the individuals involved.

In this book, we ask, How does a child born into one family come to be raised by another family? Answering that question means seeing families as cultural and social institutions and relatedness as a cultural and social practice. On the one hand, we often think of families as the most natural of social units and the most private of social institutions: grounded in biology, maintained through emotional bonds of love and affection, and the site of some of our most intimate actions. But at the same time, families also influence the public world around us, are shaped by broader cultural and historical relationships, and are embedded in state structures. For example, how we behave toward others in our families, whom (and how) we marry, who is included in a family, and even whether certain individuals are allowed to form a family are all influenced by society's laws and by norms and values that are not necessarily written down but are nevertheless very powerful.

The raising of children by adults who are not the biological parents has been an accepted practice of family formation or child rearing for centuries in many societies. Adoption as we know it in the United States today is structured by state laws and managed by public professionals. Other terms for such practices, such as *fostering* or the *circulation of children* reflect the less formal but still structured practices through which families in different times and places have endeavored to give children what they need to become responsible adult members of a community. We take a broad perspective and examine historical relationships and cross-cultural forms of family structure in this book, using the terms *adoption, fostering,* and *child circulation* more or less interchangeably.

There are many reasons to understand the role of adoption in societies. Not only is child circulation a widely accepted practice found in most societies, but it also provides a window onto broader social issues and institutions. Exploring adoption gives us important insights into the process that individuals go through to build their families and the ways that these processes conform to or challenge norms about what families are. Investigating adoption and fosterage, then, helps us understand the ways in which people imagine families should or should not be and the ways in which people enact or produce these relationships in their everyday lives.

Thus, while only 2.4 percent of families in the United States today have been formed through adoption and only 2.5 percent of children under 18 years old are adopted (University of Oregon Adoption History Project, http://darkwing.uoregon.edu/~adoption/), understanding adoption in the United States and in other societies enables important insights. Studying adoption, fostering, and child circulation is a vehicle to understanding societies and families more generally. In nearly all societies, family is a central social institution, organizing life for most individuals. But the organization of families, the meaning of family, the family's role in a community, and even the definition of *family* itself differ from one social situation to another and, as we will see, undergo frequent change.

One reason to explore how adoption and fostering are practiced in a variety of cultural systems is to acknowledge the degree of human variation in both the ideal and the actual family form. In many societies throughout the world, the nuclear family is not the ideal or even the typical configuration in which people live and interact, and genetically related parents are not the only individuals assumed to be responsible for the care, nurturance, socialization, or education of children. Bringing attention to the range of practices and ideologies around the circulation of children reminds us that what is habitual for any particular group is not necessarily natural for all human beings nor even normal in all societies. Moreover, comparing adoption and fostering in a variety of social and historical contexts points to the ways in which all families are socially and culturally constructed—even those families that we might assume are natural or biological.

Adoption helps us to see more clearly another dimension of families: Families are not simply private entities or personal relationships. The state is often involved in shaping families, and while the influence of the state on families in most societies is powerful, its role is often indirect or is masked. For example, families are obviously shaped by marriage laws, but they are also shaped by tax laws (which may protect certain kinds of living arrangements and discourage others) and school funding (which may influence where families live, what resources children can access, or how adults may invest in their children's education). Adoption often involves deliberate and careful planning for family construction, and formal adoption must pass through state or government channels. Tracing adoption patterns—who adopts, who does not adopt, who is adopted, and how others react to adoptive families—makes visible how society members feel about the attributes of families that are desirable or even necessary. The ways these attitudes and assumptions are supported and constructed in our rules and laws— those directly related to adoption and many more that affect nonadoptive families as well—underscore the role of the state in supporting, creating, and dismantling families. These attitudes, assumptions, rules, and laws influence which parents relinquish their children for adoption, which children are removed by the state because their parents are deemed unfit, which prospective parents decide to adopt and which of these are approved for adoption, which children are adopted and by whom, and which children are not adopted. Thus, examining adoption makes visible the ways that all families are touched by state interventions, direct or indirect, and makes more visible norms about families, parents, children, and government control of these institutions.

One way to think about adoption and families is to recognize that more than being parts of families, we all "do" family; through our behavior, we show those around us that we are a family, or a mother or a son or a sibling. We do not always recognize our own actions in this regard, but we more easily recognize such behavior in others—especially when someone steps out of an expected role. Immigrant parents in the United States, for example, have explained how difficult it is to have to depend on their children's English language skills to help them navigate public life after they arrive. That dependency goes against the expected social and familial roles, in which parents take care of their children. It might make others question whether the parent–child relationship is proper or whether the child is having to take on too many responsibilities; it might require a parent to reinforce authority in other ways. Adoption can similarly challenge expected family norms, especially when the children and parents do not physically resemble each other.

Rothman (2005:5–8) argues that doing family parallels the ways women, men, boys, and girls do gender: For those who are doing what they are expected to do, the accomplishment is hidden, naturalized: "Ordinary" girls and women do their expected gender stuff, and "normal" boys and men do their expected gender stuff. Most of the time, we don't even realize what we're doing or how we're doing gender. That doesn't mean we're not doing it. When called to our attention, most of us can recognize certain taken-for-granted actions or ideas that constitute gender, but many people just don't have to think about it. So it is with family:

> If you are an ordinary family, an expected family—a mama bear, papa bear and the little bear cubs born to your type of family—you don't think about presenting yourself. It just seems obvious. You don't think about how you construct the family. . . . If you're not ordinary, you have to show just how ordinary a family you indeed are. That "ordinariness" is an accomplishment. You're going to be aware of what most people take for granted. . . . We notice that we are *doing* what other people think they are just *being*. (Rothman 2005:5-6)

The importance of being accepted as ordinary helps to explain some of the practices connected to adoption, from the secrecy and closed files of many adoptions to the desire of some parents to adopt children who resemble them physically.

And therein lies one of the paradoxes of adoption. Those involved in adoption are, on the one hand, ordinary people and families, doing what other ordinary people and families are doing, even if sometimes doing it with more deliberate planning. But on the other hand, adoption is about crossing borders, pushing into the open and making visible things that usually remain unexamined and invisible, and sometimes challenging what we take for granted.

In addition to highlighting the various ways in which families are constituted, examining adoption and fostering also forefronts the ways in which these practices are constrained by social, political, and economic relationships and influenced by the cross-cutting influences of race, ethnicity, socioeconomic class, and sexuality. Adoption tends to occur along a differential gradient of power within any given society; children tend to move from the care of those with less status and power to those with more status and power. Adoptions do not, in other words, take place in any random fashion; inevitably, the pattern of adoption is the movement of children from a less valued to a more highly valued category of a social hierarchy (such as socioeconomic class, race, or nationality). In many countries, children generally move from nonwhite mothers to white families, from poorer families to richer families, and from poorer countries to wealthier countries. Although there is some movement of children in the opposite direction, the overall pattern of adoption is clearly a movement of children from lower- to higher-status families. Examining the processes of adoption and fostering allows us to see societal norms and attitudes about families, parents, children, and the ideologies of race and ethnicity, socioeconomic class, gender, and sexuality that are interwoven with attitudes about all families and children.

Thus, on the one hand, adoption is productive: It produces new conceptualizations of family and challenges normative versions of how to make and remake families. Through the process of adoption, individuals and groups have created or confronted alternative family forms: not only families in which children are biologically unrelated to their parents but also transracial and transnational families in which children and parents are of visibly different ethnicities and families in which lesbian or gay partners parent a child. In the process, adoption has helped to change norms about families and family making. At the same time, adoption follows normative social patterns and hierarchies. When we look at the circulation of children, we clearly see the real and metaphorical borders they cross and the hierarchies that configure those processes. In these ways, adoption reflects social structures and the organization of societies and of global processes. In particular, through adoption, we can see inequalities in race, socioeconomic class, nationality, and gender.

This book focuses primarily on adoption in the United States, although we examine adoption and fostering in some other societies. We will look at these two broad aspects of adoption: the ways in which adoption reflects attitudes about families and family making on the one hand and, on the other, the ways in which adoption rests on unequal relations of power. After introducing some terms surrounding adoption and setting out some descriptive background about adoption, we organize the book into two sections. In the first, we explore what adoption teaches us about family norms and forms at different historical moments and in different cultural contexts. In Chapter 1, we examine adoption and fostering practices in several societies to show how these practices illuminate the ways families are naturalized, reflect broader social and behavioral norms, and are shaped by local and global relations of power. In Chapter 2, we trace the history of adoption in the United States, noting how adoption practices have changed over the past 200 years in ways that have sometimes reflected ongoing debates about families and sometimes pushed debates into new arenas. In Chapter 3, we look at contemporary patterns of adoption in the United States. Considering the general patterns of adoption brings to light the ways that adoption is a process engaged in by individuals but also strongly influenced by social norms and state policies. In recognition of how laws and regulations are connected to norms and values, we also examine how socioeconomic class, gender, and sexuality influence adoption in the United States.

In the second half of the book, we turn our focus to the intersection of various relationships of power and the ways inequalities shape adoption processes. Thus, even as adoption involves individuals, it also involves the wider society and is influenced by systems of power and inequality. We focus on the ways in which racial discourses shape adoption and fostering in the United States in Chapter 4. Although race and class are intertwined in the United States, considering the histories and current policies related to adoption, fostering, and institutionalized care of African American and Native American children challenges us to recognize the politics of these practices. In Chapter 5 we explore transnational adoption and the ways that patterns of adoption across national borders have mirrored the more general difficulties faced by poorer and less politically stable countries. In our Conclusion we revisit the broad issues of adoption to highlight what adoption teaches us about families, social institutions, and relationships of power within and across societies.

Adoption in the United States

Definitions

Adoption in the United States takes several forms. In this book, we are focusing on *stranger adoption* (the adoption of children unrelated to the adopting parents), but in fact about half of all legal adoptions that take place in the United States are adoptions by stepmothers, stepfathers, or other relatives who adopt children to gain legal custody. While many of these adoptions are formal adoptions, some of them are actually *informal adoptions*, a phrase used to describe an adoption in which no legal contract is drawn up but agreement is made between the birth parents and those who will raise the child, either temporarily or permanently. *Formal adoption* is an adoption in which a legal transferal of rights to children and responsibilities for children occurs. There are several routes to formal adoption including public and private agency adoption, private adoption, and transnational adoption. While all 50 U.S. states regulate formal adoptions, each state has its own laws and polices governing the different types of formal adoption. Nevertheless, all formal adoptions in the United States are what are termed *strong adoptions,* meaning that in relinquishing their child, birth parents give up all legal rights to the child, and the adopting parents take over full legal responsibility for the child.

In the United States, formal adoptions are often, but not always, organized through public or private adoption agencies. Public agencies are run by government-funded organizations; these adoptions are much less expensive than others. Currently, the children available through public adoption are often older or have special needs. Private agencies are run by privately funded organizations, and these adoptions are usually more expensive. Often private agencies have more prospective parents than available children, and because of that, private agencies may apply more stringent criteria for adopting parents than do public agencies, including restrictions on age, income, sexual orientation, number of children in the family, marital status, and religion.

When an adoption is not arranged by an agency, it is called a *private adoption*. Private adoptions are legal in most but not all U.S. states. (They are illegal in Connecticut, Minnesota, Delaware, and Massachusetts.) A private adoption usually proceeds through a lawyer who matches a birth mother considering relinquishing her child with a prospective adoptive parent. In nearly all states, private adoptions need final court approval even though these adoptions proceed outside the auspices of agencies. Private adoptions sometimes take less time than others but are often more expensive than agency adoptions. Although every state tries to prevent baby selling and baby buying, different states allow various expenses to be included as adoption expenses, causing the cost of private adoptions to vary widely. For instance, some states permit adopting parents to pay for some of the living expenses of the birth parent(s), while other states prohibit such transactions. Private adoptions can be more complicated than other adoptions, partly because they often happen at the time of the child's birth. Adopting and birth parents may have recent and even direct contact with each other. In addition, some states allow for a longer waiting period during which the birth parent(s) can change their minds and revoke their consent for adoption. This often results in a longer period of time passing before the adoption is finalized.

Finally, some adoptions are transnational or intercountry adoptions in which parents from one country adopt children from another country. These adoptions are considered private adoptions in some ways: They occur between an individual and another government. If an American citizen adopts a child in the other country, the laws of that nation govern the adoption. Transnational adoptions are also, however, subject to various U.S. laws. Because most Americans adopting foreign children want to bring those children into the United States, immigration laws that govern the entry of foreigners into the country are particularly important to transnational adoption.

One of the consequences of there being so many pathways to adoption is that children are adopted at very different ages in the United States. While many adopting parents express a preference for adopting an infant, the lack of infants who are available for adoption makes meeting that preference difficult in many cases. Adoptions through public agencies often involve older children because many of the children have become available for adoption only after spending time in the foster care system. Private adoptions, on the other hand, are more likely than others to involve the adoption of an infant. (In fact, one of the reasons some adopting and birth parents choose to go this route is because the adoption takes place shortly after birth.) Children adopted transnationally, on the other hand, range in age. Whereas some countries permit and even encourage the adoption of infants, in more cases, the length of time it takes to process any adoption means that children are not usually infants when they are finally adopted. For all these reasons, the percentage of adopted children who are infants has remained fairly constant for many years (NCA Adoption Factbook, https://www.adoptioncouncil.org).

Adoption and Statistics

Although the categories that we use to name adoption and the varying processes for accomplishing a formal adoption give some insight into public attitudes and state influences, we may also garner some amount of information about attitudes, norms, and policies by tracing the patterns in adoption statistics. This information is also, however, limited. The quantitative data that we have on adoption in the United States (and many other countries) concern formal adoption rather than informal adoption. Further, because the federal government collected general statistics on adoption only between 1945 and 1975, we have systematic information on only two kinds of adoption processes that have taken place in the past several decades. States collect information about children adopted through the foster care system, and the federal government collects information about children adopted overseas because they nearly all arrive after acquiring immigrant visas. Missing from these official statistics on adoption, then, are those regarding all adoptions that take place outside of these two pathways: private adoptions and public and private agency adoptions of children who are not involved in the foster care system.

In spite of these gaps in the data, which we discuss further below, we know that the number of formal adoptions taking place in the United States has fluctuated over the past several decades. We can see from Figure I.2 that the number of nonrelative adoptions has decreased from the high of 89,200 in 1970 (which is the same year that adoptions of all kinds peaked). Yet when we compare adoptions in 1996 and 2002, we see that during this period, there have been increases, especially in certain categories. For example, the number of adoptions by nonrelatives rose from 54,492 to 76,013.

Second, we know that over the past three decades the national origins of children who are adopted by parents in the United States have changed. Although in 2000, 40 percent of all adoptions in the United States involved children adopted from public agencies (National Adoption Information Clearinghouse, http://www.adoption.org/adopt/national-adoption-clearing house.php), transnational adoption has increased fairly steadily. Transnational adoption rose rapidly from just over 7,000 adoptions in 1990 to a high of nearly 23,000 in 2004, declining to around 19,500 in 2007 (U.S. State Department, http://adoption.state.gov/). These adoptions constitute a large percentage of all American adoptions. Of the just over 97,000 adoptions of unrelated children that took place in 2002, about 22 percent were adoptions of children from other countries (Placek 2007). From U.S. Census data, we know that in 2000, 18.5 percent of all adopted children under 18 years of age were foreign born (Krieder 2007).

As these patterns suggest, adoption in the United States has been an important, accepted, and viable option for forming families for decades, and it continues to have a key place in American society today. Given the

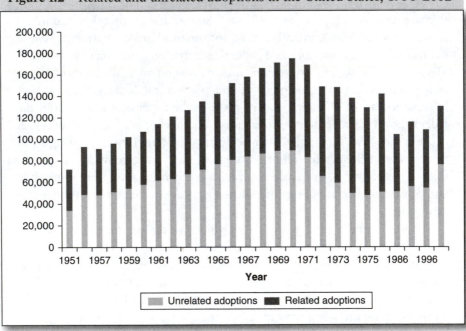

Figure I.2   Related and unrelated adoptions in the United States, 1951–2002

Source: National Council for Adoption (https://www.adoptioncouncil.org, Table 8).

history of the practice, it is remarkable how little statistical information about adoption is available in the U.S. We have never had systematic information about informal adoption, those adoptions that take place outside of the legal system. And from 1975 to the present, we have had no systematic data about formal, legal adoptions. Given the importance of statistics and numbers in nearly all aspects of our lives, it is notable that the U.S. government has chosen not to collect such information. Just as there is power in numbers, there is ignorance built into the lack of them, and the dearth of systematic and official statistics about adoption makes this process less visible and recognized. One historian of adoption argues that we can interpret the lack of government statistics about adoption as "reflect[ing] America's cultural bias against adoption" (Carp 1998:1); the government collects information about processes deemed important, and thus the absence of adoption statistics suggests at least a government indifference to these processes. At the very least, the lack of systematic and official statistics about adoption certainly makes this complicated set of processes more difficult to trace and understand.

In the absence of official statistics, other agencies have attempted to fill in some of the gaps. Several nonprofit and private agencies have worked to collect information about adoption and to act as resources on the trends, outcomes, and issues surrounding adoption. Most of these have specific agendas regarding adoption. For example, the National Council for Adoption (NCFA) has compiled separate sources of statistics into more comprehensive summaries of adoptions in recent years. The NCFA describes itself as an "adoption advocate" and as "a research, education, and advocacy organization whose mission is to promote the well-being of children, birth parents, and adoptive families by advocating for the positive option of adoption" (NCFA, https://www.adoptioncouncil.org/). Acknowledging this advocacy stance is important because the NCFA is most likely to collect adoption information that will further its goals. We get other information about adoptions from a few national sample surveys of families and households that include some information about adoption (such as the National Survey of Family Growth) and from the U.S. Census, which in 2000 added a new category for household members, "adopted son/daughter." While these surveys and censuses have provided useful data, because their focus is not adoption, the information we can garner from them is limited.

Adoption has been called "quiet migration." Indeed, the absence of data about this process has made the movement of children across family, state, and national boundaries difficult even to trace. In addition, of course, those involved in adoption have not always welcomed public scrutiny of their lives.

As we will see, American adoption often—especially in the past—was meant to mirror "normal" (read: biological) family making. Through the matching of children and adopting parents, those involved tried to make new families look like biological families. In recent years, the opening of adoption records and the large number of transnational adoptions have made some adoptions, at least, more visible. Families made through adoption may look like other families, or they may not. Either way, as we will see, adoption challenges our notions of how families can or should be created. Exploring how children circulate among families in other societies also challenges us to think about the processes involved in family building and reorganization. In Chapter 1, we do just that: examine the ways that children move out of and into families in several societies. This cross-cultural examination enables us to see how the practice, acceptance, and even meaning of adoption or child circulation varies from place to place and is related to ideas and norms about family, children, and parenting.

1

Adoption Across Cultures

A doption and fosterage are social practices, spread widely across the globe and throughout different historical periods. What is the significance of understanding adoption in different societies and historical moments? One reason to look at a variety of cultural and social systems is to understand the degree of human variation in the forms of families. In the United States at the beginning of the twenty-first century, adoptions are not as shrouded in secrecy as they were even 50 years ago, yet many North Americans still assume that natural or biological parents should raise their children. In contrast, in many societies throughout the world, the nuclear family is not the ideal or even the typical configuration in which people live and interact, and birth parents are not the only individuals assumed to be responsible for the care, nurturance, socialization, or education of children. Bringing attention to the range of practices and ideologies around the circulation of children reminds us that what is habitual for any particular group is not necessarily natural for all human beings nor even normal in all societies. Comparing adoption and fostering in a variety of social and historical contexts points to the ways in which *all* families are socially and culturally constructed.

Moreover, the practices, ideals, and forms that appear most natural to us are often embedded in particular relationships of power. In addition to highlighting the various ways in which families are constituted, comparing adoption and fostering in different cultures also forefronts the ways in which these practices are constrained by social, political, and economic relationships and hierarchies. Adoption tends to occur along a differential gradient of power within any given society; children tend to move from the care of those with less status and power to the care of those with more status and power. Local political-economic relationships and social relationships are thus crucial to understanding adoption, but local arenas are always embedded in broader sets of relationships including a global balance of power. As much as adoption may be framed as personal and intensely emotional, analyzing child circulation encourages an attentiveness to the ways in which the movement of children is culturally and socially constituted and embedded in broader contexts of politics and power.

In this chapter, we describe a range of fostering and adoption practices by focusing on three settings: one in which fostering and adoption are prevalent and preferred (here using the west African countries of Benin and Cameroon as our examples), a second in which child circulation is frequent but not necessarily preferred (using the Andean South American countries of Bolivia, Ecuador, and Peru as our examples), and a third in which formal adoption is discouraged and infrequent but the care of orphans is valued (using the Middle Eastern countries of Egypt and Lebanon as our examples). We then draw on these examples to examine three assumptions held by many Americans: that sexual reproduction is the natural basis for family, that birth/genetic parents are solely responsible for children or the most appropriate people to raise children, and that fostering and adoption are simply individual choices made outside of any social and historical context. Each case gives a snapshot of the particular configurations of practices and ideologies around child circulation, and family more generally, at the turn of the twenty-first century.

Ethnographic Cases

The Preference for Fostering in West Africa

Although fostering is often thought of as a response to unusual circumstances or as a last resort for dealing with poverty or infertility, fostering and adoption in some societies are desired, expected, and a significant part of an array of practices through which most children are raised. Throughout most regions of west Africa, people have considered fostering to be the best way of raising children. Much of the scholarship on the circulation of children in west Africa has focused on fostering, which exists outside of any state-controlled transfer of children (as in adoption), and on the highly structured local understandings of who has rights to and responsibilities for raising children. We focus on the case of the Baatombu, French-speaking peasants in the multiethnic region of Borgu in northeastern Benin and northwestern Nigeria, who have until very recently downplayed the importance of biological parenthood and celebrated social parenthood. We also integrate information from other regions in western Africa, including the multiethnic Christian community of Mbondossi in east Cameroon and the Mende ethnic group of Sierra Leone, to provide a portrait of cultural groups in which fostering has been not only quite common but also preferred.

By the end of the twentieth century, about 30 percent of Baatombu children were raised outside of their birth or natal families, but in the recent

Figure 1.1   In some western African nations (such as Sierra Leone, Ghana, Benin, Nigeria, and Cameroon), child fosterage is a frequent and accepted practice. In parts of northern Africa and the Middle East (such as Egypt, Lebanon, and Turkey), child fosterage and adoption are not common.

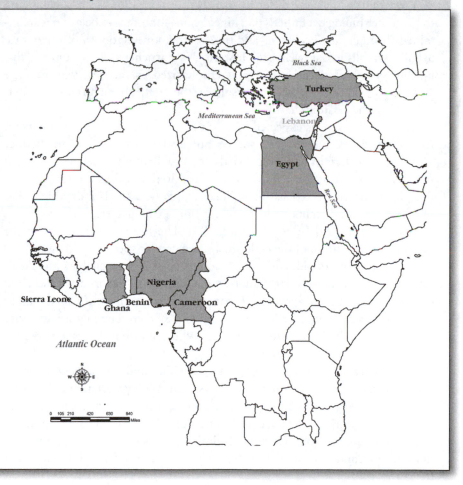

past, nearly all children circulated to homes other than those of their natal families. In fact, the Baatombu do not have a term that distinguishes between biological and social parents; thus, the distinction between foster or social parents and biological or birth parents is an analytical one used by scholars, not by the Baatombu themselves. Of the 150 people in the older generation whom anthropologist Erdmute Alber interviewed in the 1990s, only 2 had lived exclusively with their birth parents (2004b:36). Although the rates of fosterage are falling, as we discuss further below, the Baatombu continue to circulate children far more frequently than do people in the contemporary United States.

In this area of western Africa, both birth parents and foster parents are part of a broad kinship system. Birth relationships are recognized and used to determine who has a claim to the child. Because patrilineality, or tracing relationships through the father's male ancestors, is the guiding principle that separates people into different social groups, a child is seen as belonging to his or her biological father's patrilineal clan—and this association is maintained throughout life. But in addition to this kin relationship, others are usually established as well, and fostering is particularly important in this kinship system. Indeed, fosterage is emphasized as the best way to raise children, and it is this belief that results in the relatively high rates of fostering among the Baatombu.

The foster parent is expected to teach a child how to be a good person: to respect elders and to have shame but also to have confidence (Alber 2004a:41). Fostering is preferred partly because Baatombu believe that birth parents act too leniently with their own children and thus are less capable than foster parents of educating children. Usually, a single individual takes on the duties and rights of foster parenting: A man fosters a boy, and a woman fosters a girl (Alber 2003:492–93). The foster parent takes on the rearing and education of the child, including gender-specific tasks, when the child is 3 to 6 years old. Although a foster parent often enables a child to attend school, a more important responsibility is to ensure that the child eventually marries an appropriate partner. Girls usually leave fosterage at marriage, whereas boys leave at around age 16 when they migrate to a city for wage labor. Thus, it is foster parents who are primarily responsible for moving a child into adulthood.

Foster parents are usually related to the child, and the process of establishing a foster parent relationship draws from both paternal and maternal kin ties and determines the roles and connections of both biological and social kin networks. When she is about to give birth, a woman goes to her natal family's household. Once the child is born, her husband's family visits her and the child. Usually the husband's sister brings gifts and declares that the child is of the husband's clan. The child is then considered the property of his or her paternal aunt, who has the right to foster the child or to allow someone else to foster him or her. Baatombu parents do not offer their children to others, but they traditionally do not have the right to refuse requests for one of their children. In most cases, a close relative requests a child and is understood to have certain rights to the child. At least in rural communities, for a birth parent to deny a request is antisocial and dishonorable for the birth parents and for the adult who is turned down.

Thus, the circulation of children is quite common and socially valued, and the role of biological parents in the lives of children is not always straightforward. As in many other parts of west Africa, the Baatombu often deny or hide birth relationships rather than celebrating them, emphasizing instead the (social) mother or (social) father as the most significant person in the life of the child. At the same time, some birth parents express ambivalence about relinquishing their children. In Baatombu, children are not told who their biological parents are, and people must deny their birth relationships in public. The appropriate behavior between biological parents and children is shame, distance, and avoidance (Alber 2004b:44). Ideally, even a few hours after birth, biological parents express emotional distance from a child. In spite of this, people see biological parenthood "as something especially valuable" (Alber 2004b:42). Alber acknowledges, "Many people told me very emotional stories about how and when they came to learn the names and identities of their biological parents. I was told numerous stories about little gestures or little gifts offered secretly by biological parents to their children" (2004b:42). Baatombu say that children adapt easily to their foster parents, and people give attention to demonstrating that the foster parents are the "real, potent, and preferred parents" (Alber 2004b:34). But birth parents may not always completely give up their children. Thus, a child fostered by his or her father's brother, and living in the same compound or village, may receive food, attention, and little gifts from two sets of parents.

The Baatombu describe fostering as simply the best way of raising a child, and scholars have long interpreted fostering as a way to lessen the financial burden of raising children. More recently, scholars have analyzed fostering in west Africa as a way for women to access crucial emotional and economic support, to maintain the balance of power within a marriage, and to enhance the mother's lineal ties (Alber 2004a; Notermans 2004). Women move to their husbands' households after marriage, but they are still considered part of their own clans. Because women usually relinquish the first few children to whom they give birth, they must build social and emotional connections with members of their own clan through other means. Even though a woman gives up many of her birth children, she may foster the children of her brothers. Her foster children accompany her and "belong" to her in a way that her birth children do not. Catrien Notermans (2004:50) argues, moreover, that among the Mbondossi in east Cameroon, a married woman tries to balance the number of foster children from her own lineage with the number of foster children from her husband's lineage. Madeleine, a 29-year-old woman who cares for seven children (three birth boys and four foster daughters), states,

> Since all the children I got are boys, I asked my brother to give me a girl. Since the other girls are from my husband's side, I wanted to have a girl of my own. I needed a child from my own side to keep balance in marriage. I do not like to work only for my husband's family. I also want my family to eat from the pot. My brother accepted and he gave me a girl. (Notermans 2004:58–59)

In this culture, a lack of solidarity and emotional support characterizes spousal relationships, in contrast to the intimacy between brothers and sisters. Patterns of fostering reflect these differences.

Having a foster child gives a man or woman access to that child's labor, but fostering a child is not simply about being able to ask the child to help with any of the innumerable jobs around a rural household, such as carrying water, helping with agricultural tasks, and cooking food. A greater advantage—perhaps especially for a young wife, living among her husband's clan—is that a child offers an intimacy of connection with her own clan. All of a woman's birth children belong to another clan, that of her husband, and most of her children are fostered by others, but her foster children are from her own clan and belong exclusively to her (Alber 2003:494, 2004b:37–38). Fostering is thus tied into a wide array of gender and generational relationships and is at once assumed as normative and is used to navigate social relationships. At least in west Africa, fostering may be more about bringing a child *into* a household or kin group than about sending a child out of one (Notermans 2004:50).

At the same time, social, political, and economic shifts within society as a whole have affected fostering practices and ideals. Children are still transferred from rural villages to towns, but urban children generally are no longer fostered, and are not demanded, by their relatives living in rural areas of east Cameroon. Moreover, when children from rural areas are fostered in cities, social parents may provide food and shelter without taking care of all expenses or may fund a child's formal education in compensation for their labor in the household. In short, children are no longer seen as "belonging" to the foster parents in urban contexts (Alber 2004a:43). As alternative ideals concerning the relationship between biological parents and children become more popular and as shifting social, economic, and political circumstances value urban occupations more highly than rural agricultural pursuits, parents in rural areas may not always follow the traditional system either. Although birth parents "do not dare deny the demand for a child" (Alber 2004a:43), they may send their biological children to school and integrate foster children into agricultural or household labor regimes, as we discuss further below.

The Commonality of Child Circulation in the Andes

In the Andes (see Figure 1.2), fostering is not preferred, but it is an accepted practice widely distributed among rural and urban populations. Fosterage, and more generally the production of relatedness among people, is discussed by several anthropologists (Leinaweaver 2007, 2008; Van Vleet 2002, 2008; Walmsley 2008; Weismantel 1995). As Weismantel (1995:694–95) suggests, for the people of Zumbagua, Ecuador, kinship is created through "ingesting food and drink, sharing emotional states with individuals or spirits, being in close physical proximity to people or objects." An adult can produce relatedness by raising or caring for a child over the course of many months or years. For many native Andeans, including the Quechua-speaking peasants with whom Van Vleet has conducted research in the region of Sullk'ata, Bolivia, the question of who is related to whom is determined by everyday activities such as eating the same food, working on the same plot of land, or sharing the same living space. About 10 percent of families in the rural communities of Sullk'ata were in some way engaged in the circulation of children, giving a child or lending a child to another person. Very few of those involved in fostering enter into a legal or contractual agreement or go through a state or private adoption agency.

Sullk'atas often distinguish between what they see as a more permanent transfer, "to give" (*quy*, Quechua) a child, and a more temporary transfer, "to lend" (*mañay*, Quechua) a child (Van Vleet 2008:64–65). Giving a child may take various forms, but in most cases, the birth parents no longer perform the practices, such as feeding a child, that establish and maintain relatedness. Sometimes giving a child occurs because of extreme circumstances such as the death or injury of a parent. In contrast, a child may be lent to his or her grand-parents once they no longer have their own children at home to help with the household chores and to bring liveliness into the household. Although some-times glossed as "adoption" (*adoptar*, Spanish), Sullk'atas use the Quechua term *wawachakuy* (literally, "to make a child into a son or daughter") to describe the processes through which adults care for a child and make the child into kin. Wawachakuy results in both material and social relatedness. A child who is not raised by a birth parent nevertheless becomes a daughter or

Figure 1.2   In the Andes (of Ecuador, Peru, and Bolivia), children may be cared for by adults who are not their birth parents. In these informal fostering arrangements, children often recognize both birth parents and foster parents as related.

son by receiving food from another adult. Sometimes, lending a child is temporary, but the relationship that is established through wawachakuy may last far longer than the child's residence in a particular household.

For example, Teresa has been cared for, fed, and clothed by Antonia and her husband Faustino since she was an infant. Antonia and Faustino were unable to have a child of their own and so were very willing to take on the task of raising Teresa when her birth mother (Antonia's sister Leonarda) fell ill. Leonarda remained in the hospital for several weeks; she was too sick to care for her five older children, much less an infant. She gave her infant daughter to her sister Antonia. Leonarda said, at least in retrospect, that she gave the baby to her sister in hopes that Antonia and Faustino would stop fighting over their inability of have children and remain together. Raised primarily in the city of Cochabamba, Teresa recognizes Antonia and Faustino as her parents by addressing them as "Mother" and "Father." Although she knows that Leonarda gave birth to her, Teresa calls Leonarda "Aunt" and Nelson "Uncle." Teresa lives with Antonia and Faustino and helps Antonia sell sodas and other refreshments after school. When Teresa misbehaves, Antonia and Faustino are the adults who reprimand her. For Antonia and Faustino, providing Teresa with clothing and her school supplies, feeding her every day, and caring for her when she is ill—experiencing the joys and trials of life together—made her into their daughter (Van Vleet 2008:65–66).

In Sullk'ata as well as elsewhere in the Andes, in practical and conceptual ways, a person becomes integrated into a family by living in the same household, sharing corn and potatoes from communal bowls, and enjoying the warmth generated by the close physical proximity of many people in a tiny kitchen, working together in the same fields, traveling together whenever possible, and making libations to the same forces of the earth. These practices are crucial for birth parents to undertake to re-create and reconsolidate the intimacies, and the hierarchies, of relatedness as much as they are necessary for adoptive parents.

Once given or lent, children also make decisions on their own about where to go or stay and the degree to which they have been able to "get accustomed" to living in someone else's home (Leinaweaver 2007:169). Fostering is thus an important way in which children and youth, as well as adults, negotiate their circumstances. In Ayacucho, Peru, as elsewhere in the Andean region, people may recruit a child to live in their household to provide company to an aging parent or help with domestic tasks, and parents may transfer a child to relieve economic pressures or maintain social ties. In addition, especially older children may see living in another household as a path toward socioeconomic progress, a way of moving beyond mere subsistence, a way to "overcome" (*superar*, Spanish) one's circumstances (Leinaweaver 2005:164). The circumstances in which children in the Andes or in west Africa circulate between households may include practicalities of making sure care is available to each child, but at the same time, people have diverse understandings of what it means to foster or adopt.

The Stigma of Adoption in the Middle East

Egypt and some other Islamic-influenced states stand as contrasts to the widespread fostering in some west African societies and the notion that families are made through everyday practices in the Andes (see Figure 1.1 for a map that includes Egypt and Lebanon). Here, formal adoption is infrequent, and fostering is often done in secret because of beliefs in the essential significance of blood ties in Egypt. Although caring for orphans is valued and religiously prescribed in Islam, formal adoption, in which a child becomes a permanent member of a family, is prohibited and a socially problematic form of familial relationship. In urban Egypt, particularly important is the belief that family members have and should have blood connections. Without a clear genealogical relationship, Egyptians worry that parent-child relations will be strained. Similarly, in a recent discussion of men's understandings of in vitro fertilization and adoption based on over 200 interviews with Shi'a and Sunni men in Lebanon, Inhorn notes that most men "could not accept the idea of social fatherhood—arguing that an adopted or donor child 'won't be my son'" (2006:98). One Sunni Muslim man tells Inhorn (2006:105):

> If we adopt, we wouldn't really feel comfortable looking at this child, given that he's not our biological child. When he grows up, we would have to tell him honestly that he's not our child. Then his psychology would be affected. He wouldn't feel that hopeful. There would be a "gap" because he's not our child. If you have your own biological child, you will feel differently. He is your own child, so you feel attached.

According to Islamic scripture, children who are taken in by another family cannot inherit from their adoptive parents, under most circumstances cannot take their adopted fathers' names, and cannot be acknowledged as the children of their adoptive parents. Moreover, adoption makes other moral prescriptions complicated. Although a woman does not usually have to veil herself within her own household or in front of close male relatives, she would have to veil herself in front of her adopted son—because he is technically not a male relative. A man would not be able to touch his adopted daughter when she gets older because of explicit moral codes

(Inhorn 2006:108). Thus, the concern that the child would be adversely affected is very much tied to the belief that direct genealogical ties both cause and require different feelings and actions.

Moreover, although the Islamic scriptures encourage the care of orphans, most orphans are considered to be the illegitimate offspring of unmarried persons—and thus morally tainted (Inhorn 2006:103–104). As one woman explained to Inhorn, "if you bring a child from the orphanage, you don't know its origins. And no matter how good of an environment it grows up in, it still has its parents' blood. And if they're bad, it can go back to its origins [be bad too]" (Inhorn 1996:191). Many Egyptians believe that adopting a child raises serious problems within the adopting family because of the ways moral character is linked to blood and because of the more general emphasis on blood as determining the construction of Muslim families and social place and relationships more generally.

In spite of these issues, either because of admonishments about the importance of taking care of orphans, because some Egyptians are not aware of the prohibitions against formal adoption, or because of an intense desire to raise a child as one's own, families do sometimes foster children who are not related to them. Many of these foster care arrangements become permanent. Women who are infertile sometimes find that having a child in the home, even if not through a formal adoption, eases the strain of the stigma of childlessness. Inhorn (1996:195ff) relates the story of a woman who, unable to have a biological child and mourning her lack of children, agrees to consider adopting a boy from the orphanage. For the child to be accepted by her husband's family, she pretends that she herself has given birth to the boy. The acceptance of the boy by her relatives might have come from their willingness to overlook the improbability that the adopting mother had given birth to the child (as the child was a year old at the time of adoption). Nevertheless, as Inhorn reported, the outcome was positive for both the child, who was unlikely to be otherwise adopted out of the orphanage, and the parents, who had so desperately longed for a child.

Although many people sponsor children within orphanages, some may express a willingness to adopt children. Inhorn also relates the story of a Palestinian man, living in Lebanon, who married late in life. He and his wife were having difficulty conceiving a child, and he expresses his opinion that he would rather adopt than live without a child.

> As for adoption, yes, why not?... So even though you raise a kid who is not originally your kid, with time, he'll get used to you and you to him, and he will be like your kid. . . . A human being is a human being. And I love children— any child. I can, I think, feel pleasure to have any child. Sometimes I feel myself a father of any child. (Inhorn 2006:109)

Inhorn suggests that this man's experience in refugee camps and his knowledge of the number of orphaned and needy children shaped his somewhat unusual attitude toward adoption.

Thus, religious rules about adoption and an individual's or a couple's desire to adopt a child might find compromise and allow abandoned or orphaned children to be taken into new families. In Sudan, Islamic law has similarly influenced attitudes about adoption. Because formal adoption is not a widely accepted practice among Muslims in that country, the orphanages, full of orphaned and abandoned children, have in the past been dismal places where children's lives were cut short through neglect and disease. Recently, at least one orphanage in Khartoum has been working to change the fate of children who end up there. With contributions from UNICEF and local aid agencies, the orphanage itself has seen vast improvement. Children are now well taken care of, with much better medical care and daily care by the caregivers. In addition, more children are being adopted from the orphanage. Drawing from the Islamic tenets about the responsibility of Muslims to take care of orphans, officials in the country have promoted the fosterage of these children. In 2004, the government ruled that whenever possible, children should be raised not in institutions but in families. A 2006 fatwa declared that these institutionalized children are the responsibility of all society. While some families are still reluctant to adopt children, these new national and religious laws have begun to influence the lives of orphaned and abandoned children, giving them some hope of living normal family lives (Polgreen 2008).

Exploring the Significance of Cases

In the following pages we explore the similarities and differences among the cases to disrupt our own assumptions about adoption in the United States. One of the most prevalent distinctions made in the United States in discussions of adoption is that between birth and adoptive parents. Although the stigma around adoption is lessening, this dichotomy reinforces the normalcy of parenting one's own birth children. But just as in the Middle East or the Andes, in the United States the boundaries around what is natural (and the emphasis on birth, biology, or genetics) are culturally and socially constructed. As anthropologist Carole Vance notes, "identical . . . acts may have varying social significance and subjective meaning depending on how they are defined and understood in different cultures and historical periods" (Vance [1991] 2005:20). In other words, it is not simply that familial attitudes, ideals, and relationships and adoption practices vary but that these very practices *constitute* family. In each instance, the practices, forms, and ideologies of family are based on beliefs and practices that appear normal and natural but that are also in process—embedded in changing social, economic, and political circumstances. A comparative perspective illuminates some of these.

Debunking the Opposition
Between Natural and Adoptive Parents

Understanding the ways in which families—however they are configured—are "naturalized" (Yanagisako and Delaney 1995:1) illuminates both the different social practices that individuals in various societies exhibit and their evaluations of those practices. Contrasting notions of blood bring this point home quite well. In some ways, the Egyptian emphasis on blood or genealogical ties and the significance placed on birth relationships mirrors the assumptions in the United States that the best and most natural parents are the birth parents. Most Muslims do not, however, conceptualize genealogy in terms of a sperm and egg joining and sharing relatively equal amounts of genetic material. Rather, as Delaney (1991) demonstrates in her discussion of procreation and Islam, in rural Turkey people "know" that reproduction happens in people as in agriculture: Men plant seeds in women, who are like soil, and the seed determines what actually grows. In this way, men are viewed as having the ability to create life.

> In the villagers' theory only men are able to transmit the spark of life, and it is theoretically eternal as long as men continue to produce sons to carry it down the generations. From father to son, father to son, this spark is transmitted. The importance of sons is not therefore something separate from the ideology of procreation but an integral part of it, as is the notion of lineage. . . . The man who has produced children, especially sons, shows that he is a "true" man, that he has the power to call things into being. (Delaney 1991:37)

This metaphor of procreation is linked to Islamic scripture and everyday religious observance: "The creative, life-giving ability of men is felt to be godlike; villagers say the father is the second god after Allah" (Delaney 1991:33). The notion that a man's finite procreative ability reflects God's infinite ability to create the world is extended so that religious value is placed on having children, moral tenets closely tie "purity of lineage" to family formation and morality, and a father's "authority symbolizes that of God in the world" (Nasr [1966] 1985:110, cited in Delaney 1991:33).

In the Andes, people also mark or set apart their "true kin" (*parientes legítimos*, Spanish) from others and naturalize the relationships among true kin through birth. Like the Islamic Turkish peasants with whom Delaney worked, they most often naturalize the relatedness between parents and children by linking the processes of pregnancy and birth with those of agriculture and herding. Sullk'ata women say, however, that a man plants a seed in a woman and the woman's body "grabs" the seed. A child ripens during pregnancy through the actions of the woman who nourishes her child, just as *Pacha Mama,* the Earth Mother, nourishes the seeds of corn or potatoes, allowing them to ripen. In particular, the blood of the woman is necessary for the production and ripening (*puquy,* Quechua) of the child, who is like a plant. During pregnancy, the baby grows in the belly of the woman and nourishes him- or herself from the blood that is inside the belly. The "food that is served to the mother passes directly to the baby 'through the blood,' and . . . the baby turns into a person 'with the blood'" (Arnold and Yapita 1996:317; our translation). Before birth, a child is fed directly by his or her mother through the mother's blood. Sullk'atas metaphorically link the mother's blood, circulating within her body and creating the body of the fetus, with the life force that cycles throughout the universe allowing for the growth and regeneration of plants, animals, and human beings (Van Vleet 2008:59).

After a child is born, the circulation of food and energy is maintained through the intake of food. Whoever feeds the child over a sustained period of time is credited with constituting the material body of the child, and this process then creates bonds of relatedness. Sharing substances, emotional states, and physical proximity creates a shared corporeality among kin, as Weismantel (1995) shows for native Andeans in Ecuador. Significantly, even those who are true kin, related by the circulation of food and blood before birth, must, through everyday feeding and caring for the child after he or she is born, continue to create relatedness after birth. Nevertheless, as the example of Teresa (whose story is described earlier in this chapter) demonstrates, giving a child to another person dilutes, but does not completely erase, the relationship of kinship, especially for the mother whose blood circulated through and formed the child before birth.

These examples highlight two similar, but different, ways of conceptualizing procreation through agricultural metaphors and blood symbolism; yet the differences in understandings of birth and blood intertwined with different social practices have very different consequences for how Egyptians or native Andeans understand adoption and fostering. Thus, for many people in Egypt, one's relationship to a known biological mother and father is "considered not only an ideal . . . but a moral imperative" (Inhorn 2006:95). In her research with Egyptians and Lebanese men and women, Inhorn found that preserving *nasab,* or lineage (or relations by blood), is considered to be a gift of God and is also believed to prevent personal and social immorality that might lead to economic and financial dislocation. Blood ties are thus crucial to the maintenance of society as a whole as well as the safeguarding of a family (Inhorn 2006:95). Adoption in which an orphan takes the legal name of the adoptive parents, lives in the same household, acquires inheritance rights, and has ongoing affective relations is explicitly forbidden in Islam because it contradicts this understanding of how life is transmitted and how (patrilineal) families are protected. As we have seen, fostering or raising an orphan within one's home is allowed but is rare and often done in secret because this kind of "mixing relations," many Muslims argue, creates impure and uncertain family lines and causes confusion for all concerned.

Native Andeans rely on a different set of assumptions and conceptually ground their understandings of family in the cycles of giving and receiving that happen before and after birth (between parents and children) and more generally in the universe. Although parents, especially mothers, recognize a significant connection to the children to whom they give birth, families are not limited to birth relationships. From this perspective, nurturing, feeding, and caring for a child; teaching the child how to work and to contribute to the sustenance of the household; disciplining; and receiving respect are practices that create and maintain family. When an adult raises a child who is not his or her true kin, the very practices of feeding and caring for the child constitute bonds of relatedness, and children may recognize more than one set of adults as parents, performing and negotiating relatedness with each.

What is natural about sexual reproduction, birth, family, or adoption in Egypt is not what is natural in Bolivia. More than simple variations among societies, these examples suggest that we take seriously the question of how naturalness is produced. What counts as natural is culturally constituted, yet our assumptions about the naturalness of certain kinds of family forms or relationships have profound implications for how we do or do not create distinctions between birth and adoptive parents. Policy makers, scholars, and parents in the United States and elsewhere often rely on a distinction between natural and adoptive parents and children. In Egypt, such a distinction would be meaningless because an adult raising and caring for an orphan cannot be recognized as a parent at all, and in Bolivia, such a distinction is potentially irrelevant because more emphasis is placed on the everyday practices of raising a child than on genealogy. Using the distinction between natural and adoptive family members is part of how we "do family" in the United States, and in the following chapters we will examine the historical relationships, cultural logics, and social practices that underlie the distinction between birth and adoption in the United States. First, we turn to a second set of assumptions about rights to and responsibilities for children in the Andes, Egypt, and west Africa and what we can learn from these practices.

Who Is Responsible for Raising Children?

In addition to symbolic understandings of birth and blood, in many societies adoption and fostering are linked to different presuppositions about the form of families, in particular the concentration or dispersal of rights to and responsibilities for children. As we will address more fully in Chapter 3, in the United States, both individuals and the state take the perspective that parents are solely responsible for children and have rights to children (Grubb and Lazerson [1982] 1988). In many parts of the world, these assumptions do not hold; birth parents are not the only individuals with rights to children, as is clear from examples of Benin and Cameroon, and birth parents are not solely responsible for raising children. Esther Goody (1982), an anthropologist who focuses on social parenthood in Ghana, has used research she conducted in the 1970s to argue that many societies share tasks between "biological parents" and "social parents": Nurturing, educating, training, sponsoring, and conferring a name, inheritance, or status were some of the tasks in addition to "bearing and begetting" that could be distributed among many people (Alber 2003:487; Goody 1982:7ff).

In fact, child fosterage in west Africa "works" in part, because biological parents do not have rights to their children. As Alber (2004b:39-40) notes:

> The practice of child fosterage is based upon the idea that biological parents do not "own" their children and make decisions about their lives. Rather, other people have these rights, to some extent. . . . When a child is born people congratulate the relatives, but rarely the biological parents, on the birth of "their" child.

Although getting married and having children are linked in the minds of many North Americans, in many parts of Africa women do not marry to "have" children. As we already noted, the child's paternal aunt usually claims a Baatombu woman's first child. The paternal aunt can give the child to another person in the paternal family, or someone else may claim the child as his or her own. A woman's second and third children are also understood to "belong" to others. A woman's second child belongs to her own (social) mother, the woman who fostered her, in compensation for the care and education she gave her and so that the older woman will have a child to live with her as she ages. Either maternal or paternal siblings usually make claims to a third child. The fourth child "belongs" to the birth parents; however, a birth mother does not have "rights" over children. Her husband does, and he may give the child to another person.

In a slightly different way, Notermans (2004) points out the ways in which people other than the birth parents have rights and responsibilities toward children in east Cameroon. Women usually have one marriage that is formal: They live in their husbands' households and give up rights to the children they bear in exchange for financial benefit and social status. In addition to a formal marriage, which women "will resolutely bring . . . to an end when reciprocity fails" (Notermans 2004:55), women also have several informal conjugal relationships over the course of their lifetimes. Women thus may have children from a number of fathers. Moreover, a woman's mother may claim her daughter's children by preventing the child's father from signing a birth certificate or from transferring the traditional goods or payment (bride-price) to formalize a marriage. "Fathers offer little or no resistance to maternal grandmothers who make a claim, their decisions have to be respected. Grandmothers' claims also release a father from paying for cloth and medicine and from paying fees in the future" (Notermans 2004:54). Bledsoe (1990b) suggests that a father actively considers the productive demands on the household when determining whether he will fight to keep a child.

In the United States and many western European nations, the belief that "biological parents are the best persons to educate a child, and that changes in parentage cause damage to a child's development, prevents people from thinking of giving a child away" (Alber 2003:488). The Baatombu of Benin are one example of many from western Africa in which fostering children is quite common but also takes on a diverse array of forms in which people assume that several responsibilities for children will be taken on by people other than their biological parents. It is not simply that parents are unable to provide for their children but that others have rights to their children. As we discuss in later chapters, the assumption in the United States that the (birth) parents have rights and responsibilities for the child clash with state policies that work against poor families. When struggling parents cannot care properly for children in the United States, they are seldom offered the financial and social support they need; instead, their children are removed from their care temporarily and sometimes permanently.

History Comes Up Behind Us: Fostering and Adoption as Shaped by Context

The circulation of children takes place in some form in almost every society, yet the practices through which children move from one caretaking household to another, the understandings people have of fostering or adoption, and the ways informal and formal institutions articulate with each other vary by region, culture, and nation. As much as these cases of child circulation highlight the varying ways in which we all do family, the cases also require acknowledgment of the ways that even long-standing fostering and adoption practices might change in particular social and historical circumstances.

In each of these ethnographic cases, and in many others besides, the complex interplay of relationships among individuals, families (however constituted), other collectivities such as the clan or ethnic group, and large-scale institutions such as states or religions make fosterage and adoption a site to understand the shifting boundaries of family. Although in most cases the kind of circulation we have described in this chapter might be described as informal or extralegal, since the latter part of the twentieth century, most state systems have instituted laws and policies specifically regulating adoption, or the legal transferal of parental rights and duties. Moreover, how an individual navigates these relations is constrained by informal or local fosterage systems, formal state systems of fosterage and adoption, and broader social and political-economic transformations.

Although the practice of fostering is widespread in the Andes and west Africa, we have little information about the rates at which children are fostered; about the differences in fostering and adoption practices by ethnic group, class, or geographical location; and about the articulation of local norms and state restrictions at different historical moments. This lack of statistics reflects the ways these practices, although common, are informal rather than legal. However, it is clear that particular social and historical circumstances can exacerbate the circulation of children or change the meanings of fostering practices or the configuration of those practices. Leinaweaver (2007, 2008), for example, conducted her study of child circulation in the city of Ayacucho, Peru, in the aftermath of more than a decade of armed struggle between the Shining Path and the Peruvian military. The Shining Path (*Sendero Luminoso*) initiated an insurgency in 1980 by burning ballot boxes in the town of Chuschi, Peru. A few years later the Peruvian military began waging an all-out scorched-earth campaign against the Shining Path, bringing several rural provinces and thousands of civilians under military control. Peasants, many of whom were Quechua speakers, were caught in the crossfire; the Peruvian Truth and Reconciliation Commission estimated in 2003 that 70,000 people were killed or disappeared in two decades of violence. The war also initiated massive migration to the urban areas of Lima and Cusco (Leinaweaver 2007:165). Many of the youth and adults whom Leinaweaver interviewed about their experiences with child circulation in the city of Ayacucho were directly affected by the insurgency and the economic and political hardship in the aftermath of the war.

For example, Milagros's father disappeared after being threatened by the Shining Path in 1990. Milagros traveled with her mother, sister, and brother to the home of her mother's sister, staying for three years until her mother participated in a mass land invasion to secure a plot of land. Three months after Milagros and her family moved into their small house, her aunt asked her mother if Milagros might return to her aunt's house to live. Although Leinaweaver stresses the various reasons a person might request a child, relinquish a child, or as a child, agree to move, she also has forefronted the circumscribed economic options that shape child circulation in Peru. Whereas Milagros might never have left her family had her father not disappeared, war created a context of instability and fear and exacerbated the poverty in an already-marginal region of Peru. Thus, the family had to balance competing interests: the potential positive outcome of allowing Milagros to leave the family (relief from the economic burdens of caring for children, a strengthening of ties between households that might be necessary for survival, and providing a child an opportunity to advance through education or living in the city) against the negatives (the loneliness of being without family or the desire to keep one's child nearby) (Leinaweaver 2007:166; see also Weismantel 1995:689).

Although Peruvians had probably fostered children informally before the war, and many continued to do so during and after the war, the informal fostering of children in Peru has changed in response to wider social and political transformations. In Ayacucho, the first orphanage opened in 1983 in the midst of the war—when thousands of children had lost mothers and fathers and when remaining relatives were fearful and desperate and "declined the responsibility of receiving a related child" (Leinaweaver 2007:174). The institutionalization of orphanages provides another strategy for Peruvians who, when desperate, might temporarily relinquish a child; however, within an orphanage no one takes on the kind of everyday care that is necessary to make a child into a family member. In addition, a social worker or psychologist may determine that the child has received too few visits from family members and may declare the child abandoned. Peru's Code of Children and Adolescents (passed in 1992 as Law 26102), which is derived from the UN Convention on the Rights of the Child, enables courts to declare a child abandoned even if his or her relatives make clear their intent to care for the child. As elsewhere in the Andes, native Andeans in Peru may view adoption as a way to create a family, not simply as an important strategy to overcome economic hardship. The historical and political-economic contexts as much as the symbolic and social relationships at hand are significant to the interpretation of the circulation of children in the region.

Similarly, in west Africa the system of child circulation continues but has shifted contours in response to broader economic and social transformations.

As Alber (2003, 2004a, 2004b) notes, the growing importance of formal education has affected the traditional system of fosterage. Two trends seem particularly important. First, in some areas girls are fostered at a much greater rate than boys. In the older generation, approximately 63 percent of men and 67 percent of women experienced foster care as children, but in the younger generation 33 percent of boys and 48 percent of girls experienced foster care. In one village, 63 percent of girls and only 17 percent of boys in the younger generation had been fostered (Alber 2004a:31–32). Girls' higher fosterage rates are partly linked to the ways women navigate social and kinship relationships (as we discussed above) but also reflect the increasing importance placed on a Western-style education. Parents, especially fathers, see education as more important for boys than for girls because of the access it gives men to urban and government jobs. Although less lucrative than in the past, these jobs have become especially important with the downturn in the economy in west Africa in the 1980s and 1990s that accompanied a drop in agricultural subsidies and prices for export crops. In this changing economic environment, parents allow their daughters to be fostered to make it possible to educate their sons; birth children are more likely to go to school for a Western-style education, and foster children are more likely to work in the fields (Alber 2003:501).

A second and related transformation in fostering relationships is that children increasingly move only from rural to urban areas and not in the opposite direction. The reason is at least in part that urban families have been more influenced by the Euro-American notion that children belong to their biological parents. This idea has been promoted by Christian churches as well as the colonial and postcolonial state since the late nineteenth century.

> National laws of inheritance or succession in chieftaincy favor biological parenthood, as schoolbooks and media promote the image of the "normal" nuclear family of husband and wife and "their" biological children. This influence has left its marks especially on the urban Baatombu families which share today the conviction that in modern times "modern families" (as they say) have to take responsibility to their biological children themselves. (Alber 2003:501)

Although both rural and urban Baatombu maintain the idea that the transfer of a child does not cause any damage, psychological or otherwise, many urban families do not relinquish their children to be raised in rural villages. A rural family may ask to have one of their children fostered by an urban family, or an urban family may ask for a child from the village to come and live with them. But the expectations have changed: Usually the rights and duties of the social parent are attenuated; they do not cover all the costs of education, food, and clothing of the child, and the child is not seen as a full member of the household. Grandparents living in rural villages in particular complain of this change, especially if most of their children live in the city, leaving few grandchildren available for them to foster.

At least implicitly, some of these changes indicate that foster children may be treated differently than birth children. Based on research in Sierra Leone, another west African country, Caroline Bledsoe (1990a) notes that people seem to believe harsh treatment of children is justified, saying that there is "no success without struggle." People still believe that a strict upbringing will benefit children as well as adults and that foster parents are better able to provide such an education. At the same time, as in Peru, traditional fostering practices are reshaped by contexts of political violence and economic hardship. It is estimated that 800,000 children are orphaned in Sierra Leone, a country that is recovering from a brutal civil war. Fostering was widespread before the violence to help a child receive formal education and to learn how to struggle, and during the war, fostering continued within refugee camps and when children were sent from refugee camps to relatives. But because families are finding it increasingly difficult to support birth and foster children, more children are institutionalized or travel larger distances to strangers or unfamiliar relatives. In addition, widespread informal fostering in a context wherein social relationships and norms have atrophied means that there are children at risk of being trafficked or otherwise exploited (Gale 2008). In sub-Saharan Africa, the AIDS epidemic has transformed the fostering system. It is estimated that in 1993 already 11 million children in sub-Saharan Africa had lost one or both parents to AIDS (UNICEF 2003:6). The fostering system has changed from one based on reciprocal relationships to one based on the care of AIDS orphans (Upton 2003:317). The large number of adult deaths from AIDS has meant that huge numbers of children are migrating, integrating into new communities and families, or transforming the very meanings of *parent* and *child* by becoming primary caregivers themselves.

Conclusions

For more than a century, anthropologists and sociologists have documented the wide variability in the ways people create, maintain, and dissolve social bonds, including those that we recognize as familial bonds. In this chapter we have explored different practices of fostering or circulating children to highlight the importance of cultural beliefs and norms. How an individual chooses to relinquish a child or to request a child, then, is understood only through particular cultural lenses. Often the practices of family are so habitual that they are considered natural and universal. Even in contexts in which people emphasize the naturalness of birth, individuals through their words and actions "perform relatedness" or "do family" (Carsten 2000; Rothman 2005; Van Vleet 2008). When an Egyptian woman secretly adopts a one-year-old child and tells her family and friends that she gave birth to him, and when her relatives all play along, they are doing family. And when a childless native Andean couple takes in a stranger's child and carefully feeds her food grown in their fields, cooked in a single pot, and offered from their own bowls, they are also doing family. When a west African woman requests that her nephew give her his daughter to raise, and he refuses, they do family too.

At the same time, the beliefs and values, practices, and norms are embedded in broader social, economic, and political constraints. Although some of these background conditions shape norms and perceptions of fostering and adoption tangentially, in all cases, cultural and ethnic groups are embedded in large state structures. Depending on the particular case, the state may exercise more or less control over the circulation of children. State regulation interacts with local ideologies of family, leading to unique configurations of adoption and fostering.

The similarities and differences among these cases allow us to disrupt our own assumptions about adoption and to recognize that in each instance, these practices and ideologies are themselves changing as they are embedded in ongoing social, economic, and political circumstances. The circulation of children is not simply a private affair conditioned by individual desires. Fostering and adoption are imminently public processes, increasingly shaped and constrained by the state and by global economic and political forces, even though people may experience their individual relationships, desires, and possibilities as unmediated. Throughout the remaining chapters we will draw on this intentionally wide-ranging discussion to situate local visions of how people are related to broader discourses of identity and inequality, personhood and property, citizenship and the state.

2

Adoption in the United States

Historical Perspectives

W e have seen how adoption is practiced differently in various social and cultural contexts. Thinking through those examples, it becomes more obvious that adoption, child fostering, and child circulation in general are defined and shaped by each society; what is acceptable, expected, or practiced will differ depending on the surrounding community's norms, values, and practices. With that in mind, it is time to turn to American practices of adoption. In this chapter, we look at the history of, changes in, and current practices of adoption in the United States. Here again, comparative perspective, this time historical, is useful. With such a comparative perspective, we can see both similarities and differences between the ways that American and other societies view adoption. For example, the importance of blood-related kin to the formation and definition of families and the role that children are expected to play in families and society have both shaped adoption in significant ways. We can also see how historical changes—for example, in attitudes about what constitutes the best families, what constitutes the best way to raise children, or even the proper roles of children within families—have been central to adoption practices within American society. Even with myriad changes in adoption practices over the past two centuries, there are also some consistent practices. Discussion of blood ties, genetic links, and social parenting have continued to be part of adoption practices and regulations. Throughout U.S. history, social inequality has played a role in these processes; at the root of adoption has been "the transfer of babies from women of one social classification to women of a higher social classification or group" (Solinger 2001:67).

Children's Role in Society

Early practice of adoption in the United States reflected the role of children in their communities and families. Before the beginning of modern formal adoption practices, which arose in the latter half of the nineteenth century, there were many "substitute care arrangements" (Zelizer 1995) for children. Many of these arrangements resembled later forms of adoption, but most were privately determined between members of a family or across families. These arrangements usually occurred because of family need. For example, in cases of the death of one or both parents, other family members often took in the children and raised them in their own families, nearly always without legal documentation or process. In fact, because mortality rates before the end of the nineteenth century were high (particularly for women who were at risk of dying in childbearing), it was not uncommon for children to move from one household to another. The impact of these high death rates is clearer when we realize that by the mid-1970s, only 5 percent of children younger than 15 were likely to experience a parent's dying, but in 1900, nearly 25 percent of children were likely to have had such an experience (Uhlenberg 1980:315). Household organization in these earlier years was such that the loss of either parent could be devastating to the family; fathers and mothers both made important and often gender-specific contributions to the family. There was little outside economic or social support for families that experienced such losses. Thus, the loss of a parent often resulted in a child's moving into another, more stable, household.

In many cases, the economic role of children also shaped these early child care arrangements. In 1900, for example, one out of every six children between the ages of 10 and 15 was employed, not including those who worked for their own families (Zelizer 1995:56). Apprenticeships were a common way that children, usually between the ages of 14 and 17, learned a new skill while at the same time lessened the economic burden they placed on their families. Scholars have debated how strongly parents and children in these eras were emotionally attached to one another, with some arguing that high infant and child mortality rates kept parents from becoming emotionally engaged with their children (Aries 1962). While disagreement remains, it is clear that one of the changes that occurred around the middle of the nineteenth century is that protecting the lives and health of children became a public issue (Zelizer 1995). Individuals, communities, and state and federal governments all became directly involved in preserving and improving the lives of children. Both reflecting and encouraging new ideas about children's roles, new laws were passed about the economic role of children within families at both local and national levels. Some of the most significant measures prohibited children from working in the paid labor force. The process of enacting this legislation took many decades, as reformers pushed to make child labor illegal and others fought to protect families, especially working-class and farm families, from losing the economic contributions that children made and that many relied on to survive.

These struggles reflect the changing role of children to families and society, as children came to contribute less economically but were beginning to be valued for the emotional contributions they made to families. While local regulations were enacted earlier, it was not until 1938 that national-level legislation was passed outlawing children's labor. Once children's labor was outlawed and compulsory schooling laws were put into place, children moved from economic contributors to economic losses for parents. Some states began to pass such laws as early as 1852; by 1915, all states had such laws. By then, most Americans believed that children should be valued not for economic but for emotional reasons.

These transformations in the ways in which children were valued are also reflected in shifting adoption practices. In the 1870s, most families looking to adopt were generally interested in older children whose economic contributions could be expected to begin immediately upon their entrance into their new families. In this system, babies, especially other peoples' babies, were not considered valuable. The only business involving babies was that dealing with unwanted babies. A mother who was unable to care for her infant could take him or her to someone who would take in the baby for a small amount of money. These "baby farms," as they were often labeled, might try to find a home for the baby, but homes were rarely found. Mortality was very high at these farms, and the babies did not usually survive their early months (Herman 2008; Zelizer 1995).

Adoption processes were formalized amid the wide social changes and the growing belief that children needed protection. Infant and child mortality also began to decline at this time; parents no longer expected or accepted child death in the ways that earlier parents had. In addition, two events occurred in the mid–nineteenth century that both reflected attitudes at the time and have shaped public perceptions and legal practices of adoption into the twenty-first century. The first watershed event was that a modern adoption law was passed in 1851 in Massachusetts. While modern adoption practices were still not widespread at this time, this law did set a precedent and model for adoption practices and rules across the country. The law institutionalized several aspects of adoption that remain central to adoption today. This law, An Act to Provide for the Adoption of Children, made "the best interests of the child" the priority for adoptions. Potential adoptive parents were to be evaluated by a judge to ensure that they would be adhering to this priority. In addition, birth parents had to give written consent for the adoption of a child. Finally, the adoptive child was made the legal child of the adoptive parents, and all legal ties between the child and the birth parents were severed (Kahan 2006). Over the next 25 years, 25 other states passed similar laws.

The second event, controversial even at the time, was the institution of "orphan trains," which carried children from the streets of New York to farms in other parts of the country. A few stories (taken from Johnson and Hall 1992) of the experiences of children who circulated to new families on the orphan trains give a sense of this process. For instance, John Ribanken was born in 1905 in New York City. His mother brought him to the New York Foundling Hospital because she was unable to care for him. When John was about two years old, he was sent on an orphan train to Louisiana where he was taken in by the Coco family. Later, John described his life on the Coco family's large farm, stating that he "was expected to do most of the chores." He explained, "because of my work responsibilities I had little time for attending schools." While John's name was changed to John R. Coco, he was never adopted.

Mamie, another former orphan train rider, described her experience traveling to Missouri at age 11. "We landed in Rock Port, a small town. . . . We went to the opera house as soon as we arrived. . . . The opera house was full of people who came to see and take us home with them." She was chosen by "a real old looking man who had a long, white beard and bushy white hair. . . . [His] wife was crippled up . . . bad." While Mamie was happy to be out of the New York orphanage and able to roam the family's fields, she also took it upon herself to make sure that her new family delivered on what they had promised in their contract: to send her to school. Mamie wrote to her contact, a man whose job was to oversee the placement of orphan train children. When it was clear that she was not able to attend school in her first placement, she was relocated to another family. That placement too gave Mamie problems, but she was able to finish high school.

Another orphan train rider, Mary Wagner, was abandoned by her birth mother at the age of two and had a very different experience after riding on the orphan train. She was taken in by a couple in Kokomo, Indiana. The couple signed an agreement that Mary would "receive a good . . . education; attend Church and Sunday school; be cared for in Sickness and Health; and keep the 'Home' informed of the welfare of the child once in six months."

Once taken in by this Indiana couple, Mary "had a wonderful life" and was apparently given all the opportunities that a birth child might enjoy, attending schools, being given additional opportunities for training, and traveling with her new parents.

Charles Loring Brace, a missionary in New York, began these orphan trains in 1854. His purpose was to rescue children whose lives he felt were on the verge of ruin because of the lack of proper parental oversight. Many of the children were not actually orphans but the children of poor parents. In fact, Brace argued that breaking up families was necessary to save the children. One of Brace's goals was to convert Catholic children to Protestantism, which he did by placing Catholic children in Protestant homes. However, the adopting families were not screened, and adults simply claimed children who appealed to them as the trains came into their towns. While many families welcomed these "orphans" into their families and households for their labor contributions, others in the United States found Brace's methods, philosophy, and goals to be problematic. Negative reactions to Brace and the orphan trains continued to reverberate for years after these practices ended in the 1930s.

Both the passage of the Massachusetts law and Brace's orphan trains reflected the changing times and the ways that adoption fit into those changes. The new adoption laws "required a radically different understanding of family, one that overturned deeply held beliefs about blood and nurture, obligation and love, choice and chance" (Melosh 2002:15). These laws suggested that blood ties were not the only way to make a family—and that deep emotional ties could develop between strangers, challenging an understanding of biological family ties as the only site of emotional connection. But these laws were being passed across states at the same time that Brace was organizing orphan trains. The children who were moved from New York to Midwest farms were generally older. It was likely that families took in those children because they would be able to provide extra hands on the farm and make economic contributions to the family. That new laws were being passed at the same time that children were moving via orphan trains underscores the continuing tensions and conflicting beliefs about the role of children in families and the best ways to care for children.

The negative reactions to the orphan trains were part of a growing change in norms about children's roles. From the late nineteenth century through World War II, adoption was increasingly regularized. A growing group of professionals, such as social workers, controlled the process. Many institutions dealing with abandoned or orphaned children worked hard to protect young children from exploitation. At this time, new institutions, orphanages, were founded because of an interest in protecting young children from alternative situations. Early poor laws in the United States had allowed even very young children to be apprenticed if no one could care for them. These indenture situations could be abusive, especially to young children. Children who were placed in almshouses or on baby farms had very low survival rates, often dying at very young ages. Orphanages, which would take in children under 10 years old, were designed to be educational institutions and safe places for young children until they reached the traditional age for apprenticeship, around age 12 (Porter 2002). By the 1870s, child welfare workers began public campaigns against treating children in such an instrumental fashion. While children would continue to provide their families with labor and even income for several more decades, the growing public appreciation of children's emotional value aligned with the professionalization and organization of care for abandoned and orphaned children at the turn of the twentieth century.

What Makes a Family? Contradictions and Controversies in American Adoption

As is evident from the case of orphan trains and people's reactions to them, in the nineteenth century new ideas about adoption, children, and children's roles in households and families began to emerge. These brought to light deep questions and controversies about how families should be formed or possibly reconfigured. Questions such as, "How important is biology?" and "Can placing children in nonbiological families work out well for all the parties concerned?" were debated by potential adoptive parents, birth parents, adoption officials, and people more generally. By the end of the nineteenth century, important changes in who adopted children and which children were seen as eligible for adoption had occurred.

As we explain above, in the nineteenth century potential adoptive parents had little interest in infant adoption partly because the economic costs that a family incurred when it adopted a very young child could not be balanced by the labor the child might provide until much later. Early attitudes about adoption were also shaped by beliefs about the effect of biology and environment. At that time, most Americans believed that children were born with specific traits and personalities and that the social environments in which they grew up could not have an impact on these innate qualities (Melosh 2002:39ff). Thus, adopting a baby was riskier than adopting an older child because no one knew what kind of person the infant might develop into; those around an older child felt more confident that they could know the child's qualities, including his or her moral character and intelligence. In addition, abandoned children and children of single mothers were seen as being tainted with the problems of their mothers; in other words, these mothers were seen as defective, and their children were believed likely to have inherited the same flaws.

On the one hand, the increasing interest in the adoption of infants suggests that adopting parents and adoption officials believed that environment played a role in personality and other outcomes. On the other hand, the belief that blood ties and genetics are the best foundation for family remained a significant force. Even as adoption processes became more regularized, social workers came to believe that keeping families together was in the best interest of the child. Adoptions were viewed as second best, at best. Often social workers saw adoption as potentially harmful, and even dangerous, and discouraged adoption because they strongly preferred blood ties. One scholar has argued,

> In the effort to prevent Brace's reckless child-placing policies, child welfare experts and social workers went to the other extreme and stressed the cultural primacy of the blood bond in family kinship. While they extolled the family as superior to institutionalization, the "family" they now meant was the child's biological parents, the family of origin. (Carp 1998, cited in Kahan 2006:57)

At the heart of this philosophy was the belief that parents could never love a nonbiological child as much as they would a biological one and that the results of adoption efforts were nearly always unsuccessful. Instead, reformers and social workers focused on ways to keep children with their biological parents and put their efforts into making birth mothers better mothers. In the case of single mothers, reformers believed that they had to take responsibility for their mistakes and learn how to be good mothers.

Even as government and social work agencies continued to be reluctant to encourage adoption for many decades, believing that children would be best served by remaining in the homes of the biological parents, the demand for children by potential adoptive parents grew. As the contribution of children to their families changed from an economic one to an emotional one, people increasingly adopted infants. This shift is connected not only to the belief that babies could offer parents love and entertainment but also to the belief that motherhood is central to womanhood. In the latter part of the nineteenth century, with growing industrialization and the shift of work to sites away from the home, gender roles changed. Motherhood came to be seen as the central role for women. In such a climate, women filled their expected role and identity through bearing and raising children; those who did not want or were unable to become mothers were stigmatized. In this context, adoption was a solution for those couples who were unable to have children of their own.

The Growing Demand for Adoptable Babies and the Increased Regulation of Adoption: Who Are the Best Mothers?

As the demand for adoptable children grew, the number of available babies actually declined in the 1920s and 1930s. Fertility rates across the country fell, as did the number of babies who were relinquished for adoption. Widows, deserted wives, and others were less inclined to relinquish their children, partly because they began to have access to new state subsidies for raising their children in their own homes. This change, and others, created even more pressure from those wanting to adopt and eventually contributed to changes in the general social acceptance of adoption. Around this time, adopting parents increasingly turned to alternative means to find children, especially when they found government agencies too slow or unable to match them with waiting children.

Consequently, private agencies proliferated. Adoption through these agencies was much less regulated and seldom provided any scrutiny of birth parents, adopting parents, and adoptee children. These private adoptions produced strong reactions from child welfare officials. Without regulation, they argued, "baby traffickers" were taking advantage of adopting parents and harming children in the process (Zelizer 1995). They began a campaign to regulate adoption and began to construct professional adoption services, arguing that if adoption were necessary, it should be done by trained professionals in a scientific and careful manner (Herman 2008). In contrast to the private, unregulated models, they offered themselves and their agencies as the site of proper adoption procedures through a process in which the associated risks (because of the unknowns about the child and his or her background) could be reduced through careful scrutiny, testing, and planning. While most adoptions through the post–World War II years continued to be done through private agencies, the increasing involvement of government agencies was significant, if only because it was these early efforts and methods that became regularized and eventually legalized.

By World War II, attitudes had changed again, and child welfare agencies were convinced that adoption was the best solution for some children, particularly those of single mothers. Now the guiding question around adoption was not whether strangers could become kin but rather which strangers should become kin (Melosh 2002). To help answer such questions, states began to pass stronger regulations on the adoption of children and, in particular, rules about how to assess adopting parents. Minnesota passed the Children's Code in 1917, requiring that any potential adopting family be investigated to ensure that the home was adequate and that the adopted child would be well treated. This law was replicated in other states. Child welfare professionals also began to focus on making good matches, fitting the right strangers together. For this purpose, children and adopting parents were scrutinized as social workers tried to match characteristics on both sides. Some of the obvious ways potential children and parents were linked were on the bases of religion and race; other characteristics—for example, intelligence or personality—were also deemed important. Some of these qualities were difficult to determine in infants or very young children, although efforts were made to determine them from what was known about the birth mother. Nevertheless, the goal of these child placement workers was to construct a family in which the members, in appearance and character, appeared to be biologically related.

For most of the nineteenth century, and well into the twentieth century, social workers and adoption officials rarely placed children with parents of a different religion or race. Religion was seen as an important piece of any adoption process. Social workers and adopting parents saw matching birth and adoptive parents' religions as essential well into the twentieth century. Social workers—most of whom were Protestants—were particularly opposed to Catholic parents raising Protestant children. Protestant adoptive parents were also hesitant to adopt Catholic children. These attitudes and constraints reflected the belief that religion was innate to a child and that mixing religions not only was morally wrong but could spell disaster; even infants, it was believed, retained some element of their birth mothers' religion (Melosh 2002:77ff). Jews faced even deeper constraints, as many social workers and citizens considered Jews to be racially different from Christians. To mix Jews and Christians in one family, therefore, constituted racial mixing. Jewish parents were not allowed to adopt Christian children until much later, long after some of these early restrictions on Catholic and Protestant children were eased in the late 1960s.

Race was even more salient in adoption matches. We will discuss the role of race in more detail in Chapter 4. But here, we point out that in the 1930s and 1940s, careful distinction was made between racial and ethnic groups. Whites were separated not only from blacks but also from groups such as the Polish and Italians, and adoptions were not made across those lines. Even stronger separation was maintained between blacks and whites; until the 1960s, white parents were reluctant to adopt black infants. Potential parents rarely even had an opportunity to refuse such adoptions, however, because social workers, who generally controlled the adoption procedures, thought such racial mixing would lead to disaster for child, family, and society. Unlike religion, race could not as easily be hidden from outside parties, and given the interest in forming adoptive families that looked like biological families, white families did not adopt black children. These outcomes clearly reflected the racialized attitudes of Americans at the time (many of which have been discredited) and the belief that blacks could never be equal to whites. They also reflected a goal of matching physical characteristics. Thus, even for black adopting parents, there was interest from both the adopting parents and adoption authorities in matching skin color, with lighter-skinned African Americans more likely to adopt lighter-skinned African American babies.

Here again, we see contradictions in beliefs about families and adoptions. Such a model of adoption—creating an "as-if begotten" family—reflects two key and contradictory underlying philosophies that continue to influence adoption today. First, such a model suggests that biological kin are the only, or at least the best, model for constructing families. In such a model, adoptive families always fall short. While adoption officials tried to make new families like those biological ones, the resulting families can be only like, never the same as, biological families. Second, adoption and other officials—reflecting the beliefs of many lay Americans—believed that children were sometimes better off in adoptive families than in birth families. Social workers' efforts to create a family whose members "fit" together suggests a strong belief in social engineering, that "what nature has denied, adoption can achieve" (Melosh 2002:52). The power of science and the human ability to overcome nature is apparent in this ideology. While nature might be better at making families, those involved in regulating adoption and those actually involved in matching parents and children argued that if the process were closely regulated and monitored, the best outcomes could be achieved (Herman 2008).

Adoption Secrecy in the Formation of As-If Families

One of the ways in which we can observe the goal of and interest in making adoptive families as much like biological families as possible in the late nineteenth and early twentieth centuries is an examination of the documents of the adoption process. This documentation reflects and signals a major difference from adoptions and child circulation in other societies, such as Bolivia or western Africa. The first change happened in the nineteenth century when, in an attempt to protect the new family from any outside influence, U.S.

states began to sever all legal ties between birth parents and children when adoption took place. A further step was changing the documents surrounding birth to reflect the legal status of the adopting parents. Birth certificates were changed, the names of birth parents removed, and the names of the adopting parents substituted for the parents' names. In this way, adopted children looked, at least legally, just like biological children.

To protect adoptive families, and reflecting the ways that adoption was viewed by many as second best, adoption, agencies tried to prevent outsiders from gaining access to adoption records. By the 1940s, adoption records—both those at adoption agencies and those in the court system—began to be sealed, but only to outsiders. Those involved in the adoption—birth parents, adoptees, and adoptive parents—were still allowed access to these records and information. In this way, the adoption process was kept confidential. At the same time, adoption officials believed that it was important for adoptees and adoptive parents to have access to adoption records. This information, they believed, would allow a better understanding of the child and allow the new family to make future plans. It was only later, in the 1950s, that the adoption process took on an air of secrecy. Adoption officials began to believe that it was best for all involved to seal adoption records from everyone, denying access to identifying information to adoptees, adopting parents, and birth parents alike. This change, from confidentiality to secrecy, was an important one, and efforts to distinguish these two approaches continue in adoption circles and in the U.S. courts today. The change occurred for many reasons and mirrored the change in the clientele of adoption agencies. While once many of the mothers who placed children for adoption were married, by the 1950s, 90 percent of those who placed children for adoption were unmarried women, often of higher socioeconomic class than earlier birth parents (Melosh 2002:126ff). Because of the stigma of premarital pregnancy, these young women and their families wanted secrecy. And because there were fewer children available for adoption than there were families looking to adopt, agencies bowed to that pressure and assured these women secrecy surrounding the relinquishment and adoption process. Secrecy was also promoted as a sign of the agency workers' professionalism, a way to underscore that they could handle adoption in a proper way. The new emphasis on secrecy also reflected social workers' increasing dependency on psychoanalytic theories. While there were contradictions in these theories, some argued that secrecy would allow the adoptee to adjust to his or her new life and family more easily (Carp 1998). This secrecy was part of adoption into the 1970s. As we will see, changes in American society and in adoption were central to major shifts in how adoptions proceeded after that decade. By the early 1980s, most people involved in adoption did not believe maintaining secrecy allowed for healthy adjustment to relinquishment or adoption.

Adoption practices rested on widespread American beliefs in the biological family as the best kind of family; from this starting point came efforts to make adoptive families that seemed to mirror biological families as much as possible and decisions that it was best for all concerned that adoptions be final, with ties to birth parents cut. We have seen, from the examples in Chapter 1, that these beliefs are not shared by all societies. But as we will see in the following chapters, these beliefs, which continue to be prevalent in the United States and other Western societies, have had an impact on adoption practices today around the world.

Making Families Through Adoption in the Postwar Period

Even as Americans came to believe that children needed protection, and as adoption became increasingly common, the desire and needs of couples wanting to adopt attracted more and more attention and led to further changes in adoption processes. Especially after World War II, adoption rates began to climb steeply. This upswing reflected major social changes in the United States and even across the world. In all ages and groups, fertility rates increased; significantly for adoption, births outside of marriage also climbed, from 130,000 births in 1948 to 200,000 in 1958. At the same time, having a proper family (an image that usually included children and a suburban house) became an even stronger social norm. A poll taken in 1950 found that only 10 percent of Americans believed that an unmarried person could be happy (Coontz 1992:28). And children were expected to be a central—even compulsory—part of the lives of most adults. On average, women in the 1950s had between three and four children, an unprecedentedly high number for the twentieth century.

In this environment, wherein children were a sign of a flourishing family and nation, childlessness became even more stigmatized. "Childless adults no longer appeared merely unfortunate or selfish; they were vilified as downright un-American" (May 1995:127). Couples who could not bear biological children increasingly turned to adoption. The growing number of births outside of marriage, the continuing stigma attached to single motherhood, and the greater demand for children by childless couples combined to produce a situation that made adoption seem relevant and necessary. Adoption began to take on increased legitimacy as an alternative way to construct families, and adoption rates began to climb steeply. There were about 16,000 formal adoptions in the United States in 1937, but that number had risen to 91,000 by 1945 and eventually climbed to 175,000 in 1970, the peak year for adoptions in the nation (Kahan 2006:52). Many saw adoption as the best solution, a remedy for several problems at once: a way for (unmarried) birth mothers to remedy their mistakes, a solution for couples who were unable to have biological children, and a way to find loving homes for children born outside of proper homes and families.

At the same time that child welfare workers and the public more generally grew to accept adoption more readily, adoption was increasingly regulated and more closely linked to ideals of the family. After World War II, more adoptions took place through official agencies rather than private sources. In 1945, only a quarter of adoptions were conducted through official agencies; about half of them were agency regulated in 1951, and by 1971, about 80 percent went through official adoption agencies (Melosh 2002:108). As adoptions became increasingly regulated, adoption reflected an increasingly narrow view of the shape of a proper family. When we look at who was adopting in the 1950s and 1960s, we see a glimpse of the ideal family norm: "Typical adoptive parents were white, married (for the first time), in their mid-thirties, infertile for a physical reason, active in their church, close to their families, psychologically well-adjusted, and consisted of mothers who planned to stay home with the child and parents who shared the adoptee's religion" (Kahan 2006:61). As Gill (2002:162) argues, "these agencies and their social workers were involved in actively shaping families according to the ideal norm of the day. This work encompassed 'perhaps the most ambitious program of social engineering (in its perfectionism if not its scale) seen in twentieth century America.'" Under an ideology of "family by design" (Herman 2008), agency workers could decide who would make an ideal parent, what kind of child was adoptable, and which adults were unacceptable as parents.

The efforts in social engineering were at least in part about the adopted children as well. From the perspective of social workers, children might have been born into adverse circumstances but could be made into good citizens and family members through adoption. This belief signaled the decline of eugenics and a newly developing belief that environment could have a major impact on a child's outcome. This belief also fit well with an increased interest in adoptions taking place as early as possible in a child's life. By 1951, 70 percent of adopted children were under the age of one (Kahan 2006:62). Parents and social workers believed that by adopting very young children, the adopting families could have maximum influence on the children. These changes reflected changing attitudes about birth mothers as well, at least white birth mothers. In the past, single pregnant women were seen as deviant, their behavior reflecting their innate character flaws. But as rates of illegitimacy increased, these women came to be seen as ordinary young women who had made mistakes. In this scenario, adoption allowed these women a way to return to normal society and to continue their lives. The babies of these single women became even more valuable once they were no longer considered tainted by their mothers' behavior. Babies could be raised by others to become successful and happy adults.

Adoption in the United States Today

U.S. society went through enormous social, political, and economic changes in the 1960s, and with these momentous changes in the 1960s and 1970s came changes in families and the roles of parents, children, and adoption. That era was a time of questioning and rearranging the social and political order in a variety of ways. The civil rights movement put race, racism, racial inequality, and racial justice onto the national agenda. Youth challenged long-held social norms about chastity, family and other living arrangements, parental authority, and sex. The women's movement pushed an agenda in which women should be equal to men, in which being a good mother and wife were goals no longer seen as paramount, and in which women were encouraged to think and act independently of men. The sexual revolution was influenced both by the increasingly wide availability of birth control and then abortion and by new attitudes about premarital sex, numbers of partners, and unplanned pregnancies. Related to these changes, the gay liberation movement began to take off, bringing to the public eye issues that had been rarely discussed and often ignored or even denied.

These social movements and social transformations had huge impacts on families. At around this time, divorce rates began to climb and soon reached levels that have stayed relatively stable since. Divorce, once uncommon and even stigmatized, became routine and accepted. The increase in divorce meant that many children were growing up or spending time in single-parent households or in households created through combining (parts of) multiple families—so-called blended families. With new opportunities for and, especially, new acceptance of women's work outside the household and with increasing economic pressure for women to contribute to the family economy, women moved into the labor force in huge numbers. Gender roles became less clear, more blurred, and subject to negotiation, raising and underscoring questions about whether women and men had innate qualities that made them more suited to certain kinds of work and not others.

Starting in the early 1970s, fewer infants were available for adoption. The widespread availability of reliable birth control, especially oral contraceptives from the 1960s onward, was one of the major factors leading to a separation between sex and procreation. Even those who did not agree with the free-love movement of the 1960s nevertheless came to accept that sex did not have to lead to pregnancy; that separation was partly behind the increasing sexual experimentation occurring both outside and inside marriage (Gordon 1990). By the early 1980s, public opinion about sex outside marriage had shifted in key ways, with most Americans accepting it. With control over pregnancy and birth more reliable, women could better plan whether and when to get pregnant and give birth. But another fundamental change arose from these broad social changes: A single woman who became pregnant could decide to raise the child herself. Relinquishing a child for adoption was no longer the imperative it had been. The increasing number of divorced parents meant that the society was already making way for new kinds of parenting arrangements; with these changes, the stigma of single parenthood lost much of its strength.

These changes had a profound effect on adoption. One study published in 1975 reported that among 49 of the largest adoption agencies in the United States, the number of children accepted for placement dropped 45 percent between 1971 and 1974. In New York, by the mid-1970s, adoption agencies were averaging 5 white infant adoptions per year, compared to 50 in 1972, the year before the Supreme Court made abortion legal (Solinger 2001:125). While the availability of legal and safe abortion played a role in this change, in fact the number of single women giving birth increased during these same years. The bigger influence appears to be the number of single mothers who were deciding to keep their babies and raise them themselves.

Because most single mothers chose to raise their children themselves, by the end of the 1970s, couples who wanted to adopt were much less likely to find a single mother willing to relinquish her baby. Pushed by the continuing demand for adoption, and pulled by the greater awareness of inequalities such as those around race, socioeconomic class, and sexuality, adoption authorities began to dismantle their attempts to match children and parents and started to seek children for adoption from outside the United States. Whereas once it was assumed that biology and genetics would dominate how children fared, adoption officials and workers have become increasingly convinced that even though genetics may play some role, environment is also important. The change from matching to looking for suitable families based on very different criteria is at least partly related to the decreasing emphasis across society on biological determinism, an idea that biology or genetics is the central influence on an individual's behavior. In fact, as we discuss in

Chapter 4, a 1994 federal law makes it mandatory that no such matching on race take place, and as we will elaborate in Chapter 5, adoptive parents increasingly go to other countries to adopt children. It is no coincidence that transnational adoption began to increase in significant ways just as the availability of (white) American infants needing adoptive homes decreased. One study showed a 33 percent increase in the number of foreign children admitted to the United States for adoption between 1972 and 1973. At the same time, ideals about biological or familial origins have not disappeared.

Open Adoption

Related to these changes have been changes around availability of adoption information to those involved in any adoption. As we discussed above, during the middle of the twentieth century, most American adoptions were closed and secret; those involved in adoption, including adoptees and adoptive parents, were not permitted access to identifying information about birth parents. Today, most adoptions are open adoptions, at least to some degree; it is estimated that 90 percent of domestic adoptions are open (Nazario 2007) and that birth and adoptive parents have met at least once after the birth. In these open adoptions, the role of birth parents ranges widely, including having some contact with the adopting parents, being completely involved in choosing who will raise the child, and having regular contact with the child after the adoption.

The prevalence and acceptance of open adoptions today reflect several changes in U.S. society. At the same time that genetics and biology have come to be seen as less fundamental to the outcome of a child, there has been increasing interest in and provision for allowing adopted children to find their roots and origins. Some of this change has come from adults who were adopted as children and who want to know about and even meet their birth parents; they have fought for the unsealing of birth records and have been instrumental in encouraging that today's adoptions avoid secrecy. Birth mothers who were forced to relinquish their babies in the past have also spoken out in recent years about that process, with many arguing that their lack of choice was wrong. One birth mother insists, "The decision was wrong, I should have raised my son. And I will regret til the dying day that I did not" (quoted in Fessler 2003). Glory, another birth mother who was forced to give up her child, elaborates on the way that social norms influenced these relinquishments:

> Chances are the baby wasn't unwanted. It was a baby unwanted by society, not by mom. You couldn't be an unwed mother. Motherhood was synonymous

with marriage. If you weren't married, your child was a bastard, and those terms were used. I think I'm like many other women who thought, 'It may kill me to do this, but my baby is going to have what everybody keeps saying is best for him.' It's not because the child wasn't wanted. There would have been nothing more wonderful than to come home with my baby. (Fessler 2007:11)

Hearing from birth mothers is important, and as Glory's statement makes clear, changes in the social environment have played a role. With an increasing interest in identities and the ways that new technology, particularly the Internet, have made finding people much easier, searching for birth parents has taken new routes. Many believe that secrecy is neither healthy for adoptees nor easy to maintain in this new age. But birth parents have played a role as well. Because there are fewer birth parents ready to relinquish their infants than there are others who wish to adopt those babies, birth parents have the ability to demand certain kinds of agreements around the adoption. Although not everyone agrees that open adoption is the best model, and some open adoptions have been difficult to negotiate (Nazario 2007), open adoption now tends to be the rule. Most people accept that model as the likely one for the adoption of an infant in the United States.

Conclusions

We can see from the historical experience of the United States—just as we saw in looking comparatively across societies in Chapter 1—that adoption both reflects and influences attitudes and beliefs about family and children. Thus, the major changes that adoption has undergone in the United States mirror the larger societal changes that affect all individuals, families, and communities, whether or not they were formed by adoption. Children, once considered economic contributors to their families, became valued for their role as future citizens and for the emotional contributions they make to the adults around them. In the process, children became priceless. In that change, adoption—the taking in and caring for others' children and taking on the legal rights and responsibilities for those children—went from a method of finding household or farm labor to a way of designing and constructing new families. Zelizer (1995:193) argues that "ironically, while the economically 'useless' nineteenth century baby had to be protected because it was unwanted, the priceless twentieth century baby 'needs protection as never before . . . because too many hands are snatching it.'" Institutions arose, then, to protect these children and to ensure that the adoption process goes smoothly.

Through the window of adoption, we can see changes in strongly held norms and values. One scholar argues that "adoption has been accepted more readily and practiced more widely in the U.S. than in any other comparable industrialized nation" because of "the peculiarly American commitment to optimism, self-invention, malleability, and faith in social engineering" (Balcom 2006:223). Over and over again, what has been found is that a loving, supportive family—of nearly any shape—is most likely to produce a positive outcome: children who are well-adjusted, happy, and contributing members of society (Stacey and Biblarz 2001). Nevertheless, despite these optimistic and positive takes on adoption, when we look at adoption patterns in the United States today, we also see the ways that these norms have always been combined with inequalities structured by race, nationality, socioeconomic class, and gender in the United States and across the world to produce adoption processes that were quite different for different groups of people, depending on their place in these structures. In the next chapter, we focus on some of these norms and laws that govern adoption in the United States today. In later chapters, we look specifically at the role of race in adoption and at the increasing practice of transnational adoption.

3

Adoption

Private Decisions, Public Influences

In the contemporary United States, 2.4 percent of families have been formed through adoption, and 2.5 percent of children under 18 years old are adopted (University of Oregon Adoption History Project website, http://dark wing.uoregon.edu/~adoption/). Why don't more families participate in this process? What is behind the decision of some parents to undertake the process of adoption? How have federal and state laws and policies affected adoption practices? One way to answer these questions is to look at the patterns of adoption today and in the recent past; those patterns make it clear that adoption is not a random process. The parents who adopt children often share important characteristics with each other, as do the parents who relinquish their children for adoption. Examining these patterns alongside of what we know about the children who are adopted illuminates contemporary societal norms and attitudes about families, parents, and children and clarifies the ways in which race, socioeconomic class, gender, and sexuality are interwoven with these social norms and state policies. In particular these attitudes and assumptions influence which mothers relinquish their children for adoption, which children are removed by the state because their parents are deemed unfit parents, which prospective parents decide to adopt and which of these are approved for adoption, and which children are, and are not, adopted. Adoption patterns reflect the larger society's norms and values as well as the laws and regulations enacted by the state, and all of these processes are influenced by the crosscutting influences of race, ethnicity, socioeconomic class, and sexuality.

As demonstrated in the previous chapter, social norms and public perceptions are not the only forces influencing the practices and processes of adoption in the United States. The state has become a particularly important player in contemporary adoption and more generally in families, children, and parenting. While all families are both private—involving intimate and seemingly invisible processes and events—and public—shaped by and connected to other social institutions such as the economy and the law—this dual position is often more visible in families formed through adoption. Adoptive families are deliberately, and often publicly and visibly, created; because a child's physical characteristics (such as skin or hair color) may differ from those of the parents, outsiders are often aware or assume that a child was adopted. Perhaps more important, adoptions nearly always pass through public institutions, particularly the courts, and formal adoption must pass through government channels, sometimes at multiple levels. Tracing the ways these public institutions handle adoptions, a visible family-making process, illuminates and underscores the role of the state in supporting, creating, and dismantling all families, whether or not they have taken part in adoption. Laws and rules often reflect the norms and values of those living in the society; tracing adoption patterns also highlights how Americans feel about the attributes of families that are desirable or even necessary. At the same time, laws and social norms are not always in complete agreement. Laws sometimes break new ground and thus precede normative change; at other times, laws may reinforce or exist in sharp disagreement with wider societal norms.

In this chapter we take both societal norms and state laws into account as we try to understand the ways that adoption is reflective of wider social values in the United States. We first focus on the role of socioeconomic class in adoption, using what we know about the characteristics of those who adopt children, relinquish children for adoption, or are adopted as children. We then look at sexuality and how norms around the sexual orientation of adopting parents have changed. We then use these patterns to examine attitudes toward "best," "acceptable," and "unacceptable" families. Finally, we turn our attention to the state as an entity with increasingly extensive control over adoption and over family more generally. We draw on two other societies, China and Norway, as comparisons to the United States; examining the state's role in adoption in other societies once again underscores that adoption—who adopts, who is adopted, and the process of adoption—is constructed, perceived, and monitored differently in different social settings and reflects differences in social organization that extend well beyond adoption itself.

Who Adopts? Who Is Adopted?

General statistics give us important information about adoption in the United States, but they do not immediately tell us about who adopts and who does not. In the following section we will discuss in more detail the characteristics of those women and families who adopt children or who have considered adoption. These patterns suggest that socioeconomic class is a significant influence on who receives children and who relinquishes children for adoption.

Socioeconomic Class: The Power of Money

Adoption is expensive. It involves a number of costs, including agency costs, the cost of a home study (in which potential adopting parents are screened for their ability to be good parents), travel costs if the adoption takes place outside of the local area (either domestically, in another state, or internationally, in another country), and others. The cost of adoption varies greatly, from $5,000 to $40,000, depending on a variety of factors. For example, in 2008, the cost of adopting a child from China was close to $25,000 (www.adoptivefamilies.com). In addition, most agencies, both private and state, and most countries require that the adoptive parents have a minimum income and/or financial assets. These financial costs and requirements make adoption difficult or impossible for some families. Domestic adoptions through the U.S. foster system are sometimes subsidized by the state, with adopting families receiving regular funding for some costs, especially immediately after adoption. The state contribution helps to mitigate the cost of adoption, but recent budget cuts in many states put this funding in jeopardy.

Given the expenses of adoption, it is not surprising that adoptive parents are more likely to be of higher socioeconomic status than other parents. Data from the 2002 National Survey of Family Growth (NSFG) give us some idea of who adopts and who has considered adoption. (NSFG is a nationally representative survey of women between the ages of 18 and 44.) Although we do not know whether the children were adopted because of a remarriage of one of the parents or the age or geographical origin of the child, this survey suggests that class plays a key role not only in adoption but also in whether adoption is even considered by a woman. Those women who live in households with relatively high incomes (150 percent of the poverty level or greater) are much more likely to have adopted. Women whose incomes are 300 percent of the poverty level or greater are much more likely than poor women to have considered adoption. Because of the actual—and even the perceived—expenses of adoption, adoption is more possible for some families than others. Income likely has the same kind of effect on adoption as it does on births: Because of the expense of raising a child (whatever the costs of bearing or adopting the child), those without adequate resources might decide not to adopt. Moreover, because adoption agencies and authorities screen on income, a family must show that it has what is considered adequate income and savings to pay adoption expenses and support an adopted child. Even if a family believes it is ready to adopt and can handle the financial challenges of a child, the family may not be allowed to adopt. Thus, mothers and parents with higher incomes are more likely to meet the necessary requirements.

Socioeconomic class may be related to adoption in the United States in another way as well. Because infertility increases with the mother's age, and because women with higher education are more likely to delay marriage, we can expect that a higher percentage of educated women (who are also likely to earn higher incomes) will be unable to bear a child when they are ready to do so. Education and income are often related in the United States, and we might surmise that education would have an effect on adoption. In fact, the NSFG showed that those with higher education— a college degree—are much more likely to consider adoption as a means to create a family. But that survey also found no significant differences in actual adoption by educational level: Those who have a college degree are about as likely to adopt as those with less education. The survey also found that a major indicator of adopting is having had impaired fertility and/or using fertility services. These findings suggest that considering adoption as a route to family building is influenced by attaining higher education, but actually adopting a child is less likely to be tied to education because a larger influence is infertility. That explanation is consistent with the finding from another study that used an earlier version of the NSFG: that the percentage of those who had adopted was highest among women who were older, had fewer children, and were unable to bear children (Bachrach 1986).

Overall these patterns suggest that adoptive families share important economic characteristics and tend to fall in the middle and higher socioeconomic classes in the United States; with adoption costs rising, some researchers point to a widening gap between those who adopt and those who relinquish children (Pertman 2000:200). In this equation, it is important to note that families headed by single mothers occupy the lowest economic rungs in the American socioeconomic class ladder. Whereas

12 percent of all Americans are poor, more than 37 percent of single mothers live in poverty. Children who live in households with single mothers are nearly 5 times as likely to be poor as those who live in two-parent households (39 vs. 8 percent) (Moore and Redd 2002:2). While most single mothers do not relinquish their children for adoption, it is from this population that most adopted children come. Thus, it is not surprising that adopting mothers have different characteristics than birth mothers at the time of the birth of a child. As Table 3.1 indicates, adopting mothers indeed are more likely to be white, currently married, and older and to have a higher family income as compared to birth mothers. When birth mothers are divided into those who were married and those who were single at the time of birth, we see even clearer differences between birth and adopting mothers, with unmarried birth mothers much more likely to be poorer and younger than adopting mothers and to have fewer years of education than adopting mothers. Even when we compare adopting mothers with birth mothers who are currently married, we see that adopting mothers have distinctive characteristics. We can attribute some of those distinctions to the likelihood that women do not start adoption proceedings until they are older and married, thus maybe having more time to acquire higher family income.

Table 3.1   Characteristics of mothers of adopted and biological children, by relationship to and marital status of mother: Children under age 18, United States, 1982

| Characteristic | Adoptive mothers[a] | Birth mothers | | | |
		Total	Never married	Currently married	Previously married
Total number of children (1,000s)	722	55,649	3,689	43,078	8,882
	Percentage distribution				
Total	100.0	100.0	100.0	100.0	100.0
Race of mother					
White	94.0	82.0	38.9	88.0	70.4
Black	(4.0)	14.9	59.2	8.7	26.4

(Continued)

Table 3.1 (Continued)

Characteristic	Adoptive mothers[a]	Birth mothers			
		Total	Never married	Currently married	Previously married
Marital status of mother					
Currently married	89.7	77.4	—	100.0	—
Not currently married	(10.3)	22.6	100.0	—	100.0
Labor-force participation of mother					
In labor force	50.8	49.9	35.2	48.3	63.5
Working full time	(27.7)	31.7	24.1	29.5	45.8
Not in labor force	49.2	50.1	64.8	51.7	36.7
Mother's education					
Less than 12 years	(1.7)	23.9	50.4	19.9	31.9
12 years	56.7	41.7	35.3	42.6	40.1
13 years or more	41.5	34.4	14.3	37.5	28.0
Mean years of schooling	13.4	12.3	10.7	12.5	11.7
Mother's age					
15–24	0.0	10.9	42.8	8.7	8.3
25–34	41.9	49.5	49.3	49.3	50.1
35–44	58.1	39.6	7.8	41.9	41.7
Mean age	36.0	32.5	26.5	32.9	33.0
Family income					
Below poverty level	(2.3)	18.8	61.9	10.8	39.8
100%–199% of poverty level	(19.9)	25.3	20.5	24.1	32.4
200%–299% of poverty level	(24.0)	18.8	9.7	20.8	12.8
300% of poverty level or higher	53.8	37.2	7.9	44.3	15.0

Source: Bachrach (1986:Table 4).

Note: Standard errors are not shown. Percentages with relative standard errors of more than .30 are enclosed in parentheses.

a. Includes unrelated adoptions only.

The Children: Characteristics of Adopted Children

Given the patterns and characteristics of those who adopt children in the United States, as discussed above, we would expect that families with higher incomes are more likely to have adopted than others. This connection is useful for explaining the findings of another study using NSFG data that the differences between adopted children and other children mirror the differences between adopting and birth mothers. When we compare the characteristics of children born outside of marriage living with birth parents with children living with adoptive parents, we find that among children born outside of marriage, those who had been adopted are less likely to be living in poverty. They are also more likely to have better-educated parents and more likely to be white than children living with their (single) birth parent (Bachrach 1983).

There is, however, very little systematic information collected about the characteristics of adopted children. One problem in sorting out characteristics of adopted and other children arises because when we write about many of the characteristics of children (e.g., socioeconomic status or religion), we actually interpolate their characteristics from those of their parents. When we talk about children in poverty, for example, we are assuming that children live in poverty when their parents' income is below a certain level. Moreover, at least one potential source of adoption information—the 2000 U.S. Census—does not distinguish between adoptions that occur after marriage or remarriage of parents and stranger adoptions. We know that when someone adopts his or her new spouse's child, the adoption follows a very different set of procedures—with marriage often the precipitating cause—than other, nonrelative adoptions. Thus, the groups of children identified by these sources as adopted most likely have quite variable experiences and relationships in part because of different circumstances and procedures.

A major change in adoption practices in the United States concerns which children are adoptable. In the past, only physically and mentally healthy children were considered adoptable. Until the mid–twentieth century, children were regularly screened to determine if they had any characteristics that made them unsuitable candidates for adoption. Today, all children are considered adoptable, although some children may bring to their new families special needs, and most adoption agencies (and those involved in the adoption) consider full disclosure of these special needs to be necessary to achieve the most desired adoption outcomes. In the past, children with developmental, physical, or mental disabilities were considered unadoptable and often remained in institutions for life. Both attitudes and practices have changed; most children never spend any time in institutions today, and most agencies strive to place all children, even those with special needs. With these changes, special needs adoptions have increased, even in recent years; whereas such adoptions constituted 48.5 percent of domestic adoptions in 1996, that percentage increased to 60.0 by 2002 (NCA Adoption Factbook, https://www .adoptioncouncil.org, see p. 8). However, this category is difficult to interpret; it includes a broad range of characteristics, and not all states use the same definitions. Children are considered to have special needs if they have a physical, developmental, or emotional disability, but also, they may be considered to have special needs because of their race, ethnicity, or age or if they are part of a sibling group. Many children who are in the foster care system have one or more of these characteristics.

The Parents: Marital Status and Sexual Orientation

A major change has occurred in recent decades in who is adopting. While only married couples were permitted to adopt through the mid–twentieth century, today many adopting parents are unmarried adults who may or may not intend to compose a family unit with a child (or children) and two heterosexual adults. Nearly all states allow single adults to adopt, and some states (such as Maryland) explicitly state that singles cannot be discriminated against in adoption because of their marital status.

Within this group of single parents who have adopted, special note should be taken of the increase in single men in particular who are now adopting. Where once it was believed that only a rare man could properly father a child, it is now widely accepted that men can be effective and important parents. In two-parent heterosexual families, the involvement of fathers with their children on a daily basis has positive outcomes for their children (McLanahan and Sandefur 1994). This change in gender norms and expectations means it is increasingly possible for single or same-sex partnered men to adopt.

Perhaps even more significant and challenging to previously held norms about families has been the recent increase in adoptions by gay and lesbian parents, both individuals who are in long-term partnerships and those who are single. In recent years, public discussion and controversy have emerged around same-sex couples and their efforts to have their partnerships and families legally recognized. Arguments about whether lesbians and gay men should be allowed to marry are regularly in the news. By early 2011, only five states—Massachusetts, California, Connecticut, Iowa, and Maine—permitted same-sex marriages. (In California and Maine, voters later rescinded the law.) The situation has fluctuated rapidly, with several states wrestling with the question of whether to pass their own bills allowing such marriages and/ or to recognize such marriages when they occur in other states.

Similar controversies surrounding adoption by gays, lesbians, and same sex-couples have developed, with states differing in their laws about same-sex couple and gay or lesbian adoption. For example, some states, such as Maine, California, New York, and several others, allow same-sex couples to adopt together. Nearly all states permit unmarried individuals, regardless of their sexual orientation, to adopt. Some states have created explicit restrictions on the marital status or sexual orientation of an adult who intends to adopt. For example, whereas the District of Columbia allows any adult to adopt, Utah does not allow someone in a nonlegal marriage to adopt. But laws have been changing across the country; in September 2010, the Florida State Appeals Court struck down existing state laws that explicitly stated that homosexuals are not permitted to adopt (http://www.lambdalegal.org). Moving in a different direction, a recent voter referendum in Arkansas, specifically aimed at preventing gay and lesbian adoptions, has made it illegal for any unmarried partners to adopt. Of course, some single or partnered gays and lesbians are raising children without having gone through formal adoption proceedings. A lesbian may have children from a previous heterosexual marriage; after the ending of that marriage, she might raise a child on her own or with a lesbian partner. There have been legal struggles around custody of some of these children as well; some states permit and other states do not permit the same-sex partners of these parents to adopt these children.

What Makes a Proper Family?
Interpreting Social Norms

In spite of the historical changes and policy initiatives that have made adoption more acceptable across U.S. society, it is clear that the adoption process retains some earlier assumptions and beliefs. From looking at just a few characteristics—socioeconomic class, marital status, and sexuality—we can see that the process of adoption is closely tied to wider social norms about what makes a good or proper family and ideas about how to encourage some kinds of families and discourage others. Moreover, the significant changes over the past few decades in who is encouraged to, restricted from, and approved to adopt reflect changing attitudes of Americans toward families and toward certain groups, some of whom were previously marginalized. Even as there are fewer children, especially infants, available to adopt, the definition of an acceptable parent used by adoption authorities has broadened; thus, this change has occurred not because adoption agencies have felt it necessary to expand their pool of acceptable applicants to find places for children needing homes but because adoption agencies and the people who work in these organizations are part of the larger changes and attitudes about families, parents, and children in the United States. One of the most obvious connections between adoption and the larger society is the way that adoption mirrors norms about family. We—the government, agencies, and the general public—do not want the "wrong" people to adopt, but how do we define the "right" family? These and similar questions are central to the adoption process because they are also central to the shape and structure of our society more generally.

Especially in the 1950s, the model family was a nuclear one composed of a father, a mother, and children; gender roles were narrowly defined, with fathers charged with providing economic support and being the public voice of the family and mothers given the task of being at home and providing support for children and husbands. There were many deviations from this norm—families in which mothers worked, families without children, and single-parent homes (Coontz 1992). But the ideology of the family at that time ignored the reality of some families and was focused on a particular ideal. In this environment, as we saw in our previous chapter, adoption was seen as a solution for those unable to achieve the family ideal. Thus, matching of prospective parents and children was important, and only married couples were believed to be able to provide proper homes.

But the revolutionary social changes that occurred during the 1960s and 1970s altered many of the ideals and actualities of family forms and norms. Easy access to birth control, legalization of abortion, high divorce rates, new laws that protect civil rights—these and many other social factors were part of huge shifts in how the society viewed families and what a family should look like. Today, single parents in the United States adopt regularly, both transnationally and domestically. While many people might consider two parents to be better able to provide economic and emotional stability for a young child, most also accept single-parent families as a legitimate family form. These attitudes were vastly changed from the 1950s, when single mothers were pressured to give up their babies for adoption. These women were often told, by adoption authorities and by the family and friends around them, that a single mother could never raise a child successfully. State institutions reinforced this attitude. Most public schools banned pregnant girls from attending classes, making it nearly impossible for single parents to continue their education. In 1971, the Supreme Court struck down such laws, and most public school systems in the United States now attempt to accommodate the needs of young pregnant mothers, knowing that a successful life for children often depends on the educational successes of their parents.

A contributing factor in the new acceptance of single people's adopting children has been a lessening stigma for single or childless women. While this stigma has not disappeared in the United States, it has changed. In the past, women who were unmarried and were not bound to families were considered to be flawed, even dangerous to society. Even without the assumption that two-parent families were the only type of family configuration that should be considered for adoption, being single carried with it enough negative weight that unmarried women were seen as unable to be good (adoptive) parents. Related to the major social shifts of the 1960s and 1970s, and coming from the feminist movements of the 1960s, 1970s, and onward, attitudes about men as parents have also changed in fundamental ways, thus paving the way for single men to adopt children. And recent changes in attitudes about homosexuality have meant that gays and lesbians are less marginalized today than they were in the past and in most (but not all) states are seen as able to provide good family environments for adopted children.

As acceptance of alternative family forms has grown, so too has acceptance of the place for children with special needs within families. On the one hand, this increase suggests the belief that all children deserve loving, stable families and the recognition that loving, stable families may be configured in a variety of ways. On the other hand, these patterns reflect the strong belief that families are the best places for raising children. In other words, these changes reflect both a new tolerance and acceptance of difference and the recognition that a variety of kinds of social difference is a part of many families. At the same time, the belief that the family is the core social institution for shaping normative behavior continues. While we may track these changes and continuities in the attitudes among the general public and even among who adopts or is able to adopt, we also see these norms reflected in the role of government laws, regulations, and practices.

The Role of the State

As we can see from the patterns of U.S. adoption, norms play a large role in the changes in adoption, but the state is also involved in adoption and in the shaping of families. While not as overt and direct a role as the state plays in other countries, as we illustrate below in our comparative examples, the American government does play a major role in shaping not only who adopts but which children are available for adoption, which kinds of families are accepted as good families, and what happens to those who are deemed unfit. The state's more direct role in adoption is through laws and regulations that concern families, sexuality, and children. Here we can see places where the state's work mirrors societal attitudes and other places where state decisions and societal norms contradict one another. In the

United States, adoption law is generally decided state by state. Thus, the rules in one state are not necessarily consistent with those in another state, as we saw with laws allowing or prohibiting adoption by gay men and lesbians. Each state determines who is allowed to adopt and the actual procedures that must be followed.

Along with its direct role, the state plays an indirect role in influencing adoption. From the historical record in the United States, we know that laws about access to birth control and abortion have a significant effect on adoption. The legalization of abortion in 1973 changed adoption practices in significant ways. Women dealing with unintended pregnancies could opt for legal and safe abortions, and fewer children were born to parents who did not intend to raise them. Similarly, those laws that have been enacted since 1973 and place more restriction on abortion and, especially, on government funding for abortion, also play a role in adoption. Without federal and state funding for abortion, easy access to abortion is not universal. While most women who are unable to afford the cost of an abortion keep their children, we might expect that there are some children relinquished for adoption because of this restricted access.

The state is involved in other indirect ways as well. For example, restricting adoption to married couples has a different outcome in a state where same-sex marriage is allowed than it does where such marriages are illegal; in the latter, of course, restrictive marriage means that gay men and lesbians are not allowed to adopt. In fact, the 2008 voter referendum in Arkansas that prohibits unmarried couples from adopting was primarily motivated by an interest in keeping gays and lesbians from adopting, and such a measure was seen as the best way to do so. Some of the loudest voices protesting that referendum point not to the restrictions for gays and lesbians but to the increased difficulty in finding homes for children now that they cannot be placed in those of unmarried couples (even heterosexual couples).

The government also influences families through its role in the foster system and fostering generally. In 2005, there were over 500,000 children in the foster care system (childwelfare.gov). Some of them are there temporarily; half of the children who enter this system stay in it for less than a year, but some stay in this system for longer periods of time. Most of the children in foster care have been removed from their families because the government has deemed the parents—either temporarily or permanently—unfit. But the standards of fit and unfit that are used are controversial and vary from one state or county to another, even from one social worker to another. In addition, some groups are targeted differently in this process. For example, poor households are particularly subject to government interventions; these households are more heavily scrutinized than others partly because they are more likely to have had contact with government agencies in their search for outside support (e.g., in the form of supplemental income or food or housing subsidies). Once that contact is initiated, the government is better able to scrutinize children's conditions and parental involvement than it is in middle-class households that have less regular contact with government agencies. Thus, the foster care system is heavily populated by children who have been removed from poor households, partly because poor parents struggle to raise children in such environments but also at least partly because these households bear more state scrutiny.

The plight of children who end up in the foster system is both disturbing and encouraging. Foster care is not usually stable, and children often move from household to household. One child in the foster system describes his experience with these words:

> I was 3 years old [when first placed]. I have been at 36 different places. I was in lockdown, juvenile hall, group homes, residential and treatment centers and foster homes, some good and some bad. I was homeless many times and ran away several times. Between times, I was in kin-care, with my grandmother. (Morris 2007:423–24)

Another young man states simply, "I was so tired of moving. I had moved over 30 times. I did not unpack my bags anymore because I would lose my things" (Morris 2007:424). It is because of the effects of such instability on children's lives that the government and authorities are eager to get children into stable families. To this end, the government's passage of the Adoption and Safe Families Act of 1997 helped to encourage more adoption of children in states' fosterage systems. This act mandated that birth parents lose parental rights over children who have been in state custody for 15 of the preceding 22 months; it meant that those working with foster kids began to place a greater emphasis on finding suitable homes for children, including children who are hard to place because of special needs or age, and less emphasis on family reunification. Indeed, after the passage of the act, there were some changes in the outcome of fostered children. In 2005, 54 percent of children in the system were reunited with their parents (down from 57 percent in 2000), and 18 percent were adopted by nonrelatives (up from 17 percent in 2000) (childwelfare.gov). More than half (56 percent) of all adoptions that occurred in 2002 were processed through state agencies. While there were over 24,000 nonrelative adoptions processed by public agencies in 1997, this number increased to nearly 43,000 in 2002, a 76 percent increase (NCA Adoption Factbook, https://www.adoptioncouncil.org, Figure 2.7). Many of these changes are attributed to the passage of the 1997 act.

But even as some celebrate this increase in adoptions out of the foster system, others lament the growing numbers of children who are placed in foster care after being removed from their families. This concern reminds us that even as adoption is often the beginning of a new family and new family ties, it is at the same time the destruction of a family, as we discuss further in Chapter 4. Adoptions through the foster system often occur because one set of parents have been found to be lacking and another set to be worthy of raising a child.

One of the most important and far-reaching ways that the U.S. government is involved in adoption is in regulating how families in general are supported through government funding in the United States. Most Americans believe it is the responsibility of the parents to provide economically for the children in the family; government subsidies are seen as emergency, short-term solutions to difficult or crisis situations (Grubb and Lazerson [1982] 1988; Secombe 2006). Such aid is miserly because it is given to families that have failed to adequately provide for their children; it is seen as a gift—or as charity—and not something the families or the children deserve.

As we will see below, attitudes about family aid differ remarkably between the United States and other industrialized countries; these differences are related to how different societies see the responsibility for children. In some societies, raising children to be good citizens is the responsibility of the entire society, and parents are given help in that societal responsibility (Rainwater and Smeeding 2003). In the United States, the family is considered private, even as the state regulates much of family life from marriage to sexuality to whether children can work in the labor force. In this kind of situation, any state aid given to families is meant to help families do their jobs better, to meet their responsibilities as parents. But when families are unable to provide for their children, these families—often from marginalized groups because of poverty or race—are seen as failures, failures that the state then has the right to step in and take control of. The irony is that in the United States, the government is as likely to remove a child from his or her family (of origin) and place the child with another, unfamiliar family as it is to give the family of origin the kind of support it would need to keep the child within it.

The Adoption and Safe Families Act of 1997 subsidized adoption, and after its passage, 80 percent of the states underwrote adoption subsidies. That meant that a single woman raising her own child might not get any financial help from the state, but if she put that child up for adoption, the adopting family would get a subsidy and/or tax break of about $3,000 (Solinger 2001:133). In a similar way, foster parents are given money to raise children, the same children who may have been taken away from birth parents because they did not have enough money for their children. As one New York judge described this system, "the further the child is removed from his family, the more we are ready to pay for his support" (Solinger 2001:185). Another researcher went further to make clear the outcomes of such differentials in child support:

> That means some good people who could have become responsible parents, if only they had a little more help, will lose their sons and daughters. But that's a sacrifice society has decided is worth imposing in an effort to unlock a cruel trap that has confined generations of children. Besides, as a result of the nation's new laws and standards, the scales are increasingly being tipped in favor of people who want to adopt. (Pertman 2000:182)

The resources that middle-class families have available mean not only that they are able to avoid government intervention and scrutiny but that adoption laws that favor certain restrictions such as family forms or a particular definition of financial stability also favor middle-class families over poorer, less resource-rich families. And as we will elaborate in the next chapter, because race and socioeconomic class are so closely linked in the United States, minority families, individuals, children, and parents are more likely to be disadvantaged in the adoption process—such families are more likely to be subject to the removal of children by government agencies, and they are less likely to qualify for adoption of a child.

Comparative Perspectives on Government's Role in Adoption

What other kind of role might the state play in adoption? The contrast between the role of the government in the United States and the role of the governments in China and Norway allow us to see the different ways states play a role in these family-making processes. In both China and Norway, the state's role is more direct and immediate than it is in the United States, but state involvement produces different adoption outcomes in each society.

Adoption in China

In recent years, Western news media have highlighted the plight of abandoned girls in China. Partly because of the number of previously abandoned girls who are adopted transnationally, there is sometimes the assumption that adoption is not accepted within China. In addition, because China is known to be a society that favors sons, some people assume that Chinese couples do not want to adopt girls in particular. But these understandings are not completely accurate. While there has been some reluctance to adopt in the past, today many couples in China are willing to adopt children, especially the abandoned girls who end up in state institutions. However, the Chinese government has made domestic adoption difficult for most couples.

In the past, adoption was not uncommon in China. There were legal restrictions on the process of adoption, restrictions that limited who could be adopted and what the resulting relationship would be. In addition, Confucian tenets emphasized the importance of continuing the blood line from father to son (the patriline). But these restrictions were regularly circumvented in practice (Johnson 2002), and while many adoptions were within the patriline, there were many others that occurred outside it. In fact, while Confucianism influenced the emphasis on the patriline, it was also this philosophy that provided support for adoption: "Confucian emphasis on upbringing and cultivation as the key to character provides further support for ties built on nurture and social relationships rather than on biology and heredity" (Johnson 2002:384). Because the only formal adoptions recognized by the early Chinese state were those of boys for the purpose of providing an heir for a family, we do not have systematic records of the adoptions of others, including girls. But it is clear from the records we do have that adoptions were frequent and included the adoption of both boys and girls. Some girls were adopted as *tongyangxi* (future adopted daughters-in-law); they were adopted at a young age and raised by their future husbands' families, eventually marrying their husbands. That practice was outlawed in 1950. Other girls were adopted and brought into their adopted families not for their future roles, but for the immediate contributions—economic or emotional—that they could make to their adopted families. In other situations, girls were adopted because some people believed that adopting a daughter might "lead in" a son—making it more likely that a woman's next birth would produce a boy.

Today, son preference is widespread in China, and it is that preference, coupled with the strict birth-planning policy of the government, that has led to the abandonment of millions of girls. But while many families, and perhaps most families, prefer to have at least one son, most would ideally like to have a son and a daughter. Many researchers working in China have found that couples want to have a gender-balanced family (Greenhalgh and Li 1995). Chinese couples may be less reluctant to adopt girls than boys who are unrelated because girls' relationship to their families and family lines are and can be more ambiguous than are boys'. But the government generally restricts the domestic adoption of abandoned girls to those couples who have no children and who can prove that they are physiologically unable to have children.

Thus, the number of abandoned girls in Chinese institutions has continued to grow as parents abandon daughters to try to have sons. The government restricts adoption because it is concerned that parents will try to circumvent the birth-planning rules through adoption (e.g., abandoning their daughter to have a son, knowing they can adopt a girl at a later time). Even so, of those who adopted girls between 1980 and 2004, less than 50 percent were childless. Many of these couples adopt girls because girls are much more available than are boys, but some adopt a girl hoping that this process will lead in a son, who will be born later. Others, of course, specifically desire daughters: 31 percent of the adoptions of girls take place in families that have only sons and desire a daughter (Zhang 2006:315). Although in recent years the government has stated its goal of increasing domestic adoption, the difficulties of and restrictions placed on domestic adoptions have dampened interest among Chinese couples and decreased the numbers of potential adoptive parents. The centrality of the birth-planning policy and the government's care in keeping the policy in place may mean it continues to be the major force in limiting domestic adoption. Far from mirroring societal values, the state has kept those values in check through its tight control over who is allowed to adopt.

Adoption in Norway

Comparing U.S. practices with those of another industrialized Western country is also instructive. In Norway, the state takes a very active role in adoption. First, for couples unable to conceive a child, there are important restrictions on alternative routes to making a family. Sperm donation is permitted, but neither egg donation nor surrogacy is allowed by law. Thus, many such couples turn to adoption. Adoption is restricted to married couples only and only to those couples unable to bear a child biologically (Howell 2006:23). Thus, the state has a strong hand in adoption in Norway.

State involvement influences adoption in indirect ways as well, and these may have just as much significance as legal restrictions on who can adopt a child. Unlike in the United States, where we saw that adopting parents tend to be wealthier than others, in Norway, we see no socioeconomic differences between parents who do and do not adopt. That is likely the result of the fact that the government subsidizes the costs of adoption in Norway (Selman 2006). With adoption costs relatively low, adopting parents represent a wide range of socioeconomic statuses. In addition, there are virtually no children relinquished for adoption in Norway. Part of the reason may be that, in contrast to the United States, birth control and abortion are legal and funded by the government. When a child is born, it is nearly always a wanted child, resulting in very few infants' being available for adoption in Norway. In addition, again in contrast to the situation in the United States, the Norwegian government is not likely to need to remove a child from a household or family for financial reasons: In that country, any parent—single, adopting, or one of a two-parent biological household—is entitled to state subsidies to help offset the costs of raising a child. These regulations and laws suggest a different set of norms in the United States and Norway. While most Americans believe that parents should be able to care for their children and thus state support is either weak or nonexistent for struggling families, most Norwegians believe that raising children is the responsibility of the entire country and that the state should play a direct role in making it possible for families to stay together and prosper.

Conclusions

We can see that while adoption seems at first glance to be a random process equally distributed across the U.S. social landscape, in fact there are clear patterns in who adopts and which children get adopted that reflect large societal patterns. Adoption has changed as American society has changed. No longer do only white, middle-class, heterosexual, married couples, adopt; parents now include people from many diverse social groups. The adoptions that result do not necessarily resemble a biological family, nor is that an important goal for most. The many types of adoptive families in the United States today reflect the ways that American families more generally have changed and become more varied; at the same time, some people are more restricted than others in the adoption process, and these differences reflect their different status in the overall society and the ways their families resemble or differ from accepted norms. When we compare adoption patterns in the United States with those in China and Norway, we see that the patterns reflect wider norms about what we expect the government's role to be in adoption and in families more generally.

4

Race, Ethnicity, and Racism in Adoption and Fosterage Systems

I n this chapter, we focus on the ways in which race shapes the boundaries of adoption and fostering in the United States. Although poor children of all racial and ethnic groups are more likely than their middle- or upper-class counterparts to circulate among households, in the 1990s the percentage of African American children removed from their homes and placed in foster care far exceeded their percentage in the general population. Prior to the passage of the Indian Child Welfare Act in 1978, Native American children were also overrepresented in the population of children fostered or adopted into families or raised in institutional settings. Yet Latin American and Asian American children of the same socioeconomic background are underrepresented in the population of children in foster care.

Although it is clear that adoption and fostering are the expected and valued norms in some societies, as we discuss in Chapter 1, in the United States where the most "natural" and valued relationships are biological, we need to ask why some children are more likely than others to be taken from their birth parents by agents of the state. Although the best interests of the child has been one of the key standards underlying adoption and fostering, the scholarship on adoption, fostering, and child welfare in the United States challenges us to confront the ways in which these practices are configured differently by and for different ethnic and racial groups. Before delving into the specifics of race and adoption in the United States, we explain the current scholarly perspective on race in the social sciences. No longer accepted as a biological construct, race nevertheless is a social category and everyday reality that shapes the lives of individuals. Then, we look at the role of race and racism in adoption practices and the foster care system in the United States during the mid– to late–twentieth century. We consider debates over the adoption of African American children by white families in the 1970s, the current disproportionate removal of children from the homes of poor and minority families, and the efforts of Native American groups to emphasize the best interests of the community (as well as the child) in adoption proceedings. We demonstrate that adoption and fostering—and the corresponding intervention of the state and removal of children from certain families—are systematically patterned processes that have long been linked to racialized discourses no matter what any particular individual's desires, intentions, or experiences of adoption may be.

Race: A Social Construct, a Forceful Reality

Counting the children in the foster system in terms of racial categories or sorting through the debates around the appropriateness of interracial adoption is dangerous. It is dangerous because it challenges some of the hegemonic assumptions about what we, as a nation, do for our children and because it questions the ideal that the love within a family is color-blind. It is also dangerous because these endeavors re-essentialize the very categories that social and natural scientists have worked hard to disrupt over the course of the past two decades. As Pauline Turner Strong and Barrik Van Winkle (1996:565) note at the end of their reflections on the ways "Indian blood" has been used in figuring Native North American identities, "dismantling the intricate edifice of racism . . . is not simply a matter of exposing its essentialism and discarding its associated policies" but requires recognizing the validity of the "rights and resistances that have been couched in terms of that very discourse." They draw on postcolonial theorist Gayatri Spivak's (1993:5) characterization of this as a "semimournful position" in which a problematic category is also unavoidably useful. Elizabeth Higginbotham (1992:267) refers to this use of race as a "double-voiced discourse," wherein race is simultaneously used to discriminate against a group of people and can also be reappropriated by that very group to resist those discriminatory practices. She argues that "through a range of shifting, even contradictory meanings and accentuations expressed at the level of individual and group consciousness, blacks fashioned race into a cultural identity that resisted white hegemonic discourses." We find it necessary, as have other scholars, to use the terms *race* and *racism* (as well as the categories of white, black, African

American, Asian American, Native American, etc.) to illuminate the ways in which adoption and fostering are institutionalized in the United States, to turn a critical eye to the placement of children, to consider how the needs of a community may or may not be weighed against those of a child, and to recognize the very painful search for belonging that adoptees often pursue.

In the United States, race is assumed to be an essential aspect of identity: Each individual is born into a racial group, born with a particular race. Race is also assumed to be fundamentally biological and/or physiological. Skin color, hair type, facial features—these are the visual cues of racial categorization. Although most students in U.S. colleges and universities might agree that one racial group is not necessarily more intelligent, moral, or civilized than another, many would also claim that races exist as easily distinguishable populations of black and white, and maybe also yellow and brown, people. Martin Luther King is recognized by schoolchildren as well as adults as one of the most important people in the history of the United States, as is Abraham Lincoln. The race of each is also assumed to be clear.

Most anthropologists and sociologists, not to mention biologists, would, however, argue that race is socially and culturally constructed. Although many social scientists unself-consciously used racial categorizations well into the twentieth century, others have systematically traced the construction and naturalization of racial hierarchies both throughout history and within particular societies. Why, one might ask, are hair texture and skin color the determining physical indicators that enable one to separate human beings into distinct groups? Why not some other physically discernible difference controlled in part by genetics such as height, or the color and texture of ear wax, or the ability to roll one's tongue? The answer, in part, lies in a particular history of colonial expansion and violence, for it was in the sixteenth and seventeenth centuries that racial categories were developed and solidified when European powers came into contact with and colonized people living in a diverse array of cultures and societies (Omi and Winant 1994; Wade 1997). As colonial powers, such as Spain, Portugal, the Netherlands, and England, attempted to maintain control within their colonies and to draw clear boundaries around those in power, they increasingly relied on racial categorizations. Because men and women of different ethnic, cultural, linguistic, and national backgrounds came into contact with each other literally and figuratively, children born in the colonies were ambiguously positioned. By what means would children be placed into different categories (Stoler 1989)? In the United States, racial categories came to be aligned with particular physical characteristics (including skin color). Moreover, the system of hypodescent, through which children of mixed-race unions are assigned to the lower-status racial category, served the purposes of slave owners who could claim the children of slave women raped by white men as slaves rather than citizens. This system has continued to be used in the United States and serves to preserve white privilege as well as the myth that race can be divided into a few clearly distinguishable categories.

We can see racialized assumptions everywhere, including in the media, the arts, and the movies. In Mike Leigh's 1996 film *Secrets and Lies*, a twenty-something successful woman, Hortense, who was adopted as a child, works up the courage to call the woman listed on a document as her birth mother. When Cynthia Purley, a white working-class woman, reluctantly agrees to meet Hortense, she balks. Upon seeing her, she exclaims, "Dearie, it's impossible. . . . I never even slept with a black man!" Then a look of horror and realization crosses her face; apparently, she realizes that one of her sexual partners was black or that she herself has African ancestry. The naturalness of race and racial categorization collide in this scene with the naturalness of parenting and parentage. The legitimacy of Hortense's claim that Cynthia is her birth mother is in doubt and later in the film is easy to hide from other family members because the women's purported racial categories do not match, visually. That the members of a single (genealogically related) black family may have varying physical features, including skin color, is common knowledge among blacks but often something of a surprise to many whites. In part the strength of the hypo-descent rule is in its invisibility, in the ways race has been naturalized.

Since the end of the twentieth century, biologists and geneticists have linked forces with sociologists and anthropologists to argue that races—as biologically separable populations—do not exist and that race as a biological category is meaningless. What does this mean? Although human beings exhibit a range of genetic differences that result in observable variations in physical characteristics, scientists are not able to draw clear boundaries around human populations based on the genetic and phenotypic characteristics (such as hair texture, skin color, and shape of facial features) most often associated with different races. The technological revolution of modern genetic science has demonstrated that there is more genetic variation within than between purported racial groups. In other words, there is more genetic variation within any particular group of blacks or Asians than between a group of blacks and a group of Asians. This perspective from the natural sciences, which acknowledges the magnitude of the human genome and the high degree of shared genomic material among human beings, suggests the complexity of genetic expression and points toward the inconsequentiality of those biological differences among groups that we recognize as racial groups.

Inconsequential as a biological construct, race nevertheless exists as a social construct. Even the potentially enlightened categories of "biracial," "multiracial," and "interracial" depend on the assumed existence of prior "pure" racial categories (black, white, Asian, Latino/a) (Frankenberg 1993; Rothman 2005:88–89). The fact that racial discourses and hierarchies continue to shape social, political, and economic relationships cannot be denied. Race does exist as a social category that forcefully shapes the realities through which people live; race denotes a set of discourses and practices with political and affective force. Belonging to an African American community, being black, is much more than having a particular shade of skin or texture of hair. Race is connected to a set of cultural and social resources. In spite of the lack of grounding as a biological category, race profoundly affects peoples' lives because racial discourses continue to circulate within society, created and re-created by institutional structures and by individuals. Barbara Katz Rothman (2005:91), a white sociologist who is the mother of an adopted black daughter, explains the complex meaning of race this way:

> It is a tangled, complicated relationship that exists between culture and the body. It is not that ethnicity, the way of life, the community, the culture is carried in the blood, in the body, as racist essentialists would claim. But the body is marked with history, and so ripe for claiming by a community. Is that so bad? Of course it has the awful flip side, the dark side of community: some bodies are marked as not belonging, marked as other.

Race in U.S. Adoption History

Up until the 1960s, African Americans were mostly excluded from formal adoption practices in the United States. Some adoption officials in the mid–twentieth century argued that the exclusion of blacks from adoption efforts was due to black mothers' not wanting to relinquish children for adoption and to the relative dearth of black families willing to adopt any such children, making placement of black children difficult. But whatever the rhetoric by adoption officials and others, we know that African American birth mothers, children, and potential adoptive parents were systematically left out of any institutionalized support systems related to adoption for many decades. In fact, very little effort was made to extend adoption services to black communities prior to the 1970s. Adoption was "the least likely of all child welfare services to be extended to black children" (Billingsley and Giovannoni 1972:72, quoted in Herman 2008:230). Because of very strict policies of racial matching, adoption agencies would not even consider the adoption of black children by families other than black families. "The notion that it was as 'natural' for blacks to keep their children as it was for whites to give them up revealed how racially differentiated conceptions of nature rationalized unequal social services and choices" (Herman 2008:230). So what happened to black children whose birth parents were unable to care for them? Because of the lack of alternatives, African Americans often found ways to raise these children within local communities through fostering arrangements.

When called on, many friends and relatives, individually and jointly, navigated difficult social and economic circumstances to informally foster children. In *All Our Kin,* Carol Stack (1974) brings attention to the informal fostering of children and other intricate care and kinship ties among African Americans who had migrated from southern towns to northern cities over the course of three generations. In this urban community, those with resources—whether time, money, or something else—expected and were expected to share those resources with their neighbors. Children were usually cared for by their mothers, but when that was impossible, others stepped in to offer temporary or long-term help.

Almost two decades later, in another volume, *Call to Home,* Stack (1996) traces the family and community members—adults following a dream or starting over again, children needing the care of a relative or willing to help out someone else—who returned to rural regions and towns of the south. Unlike many, Pearl Bishop never left Burdy's Bend, a South Carolina town, but she saw many others come and go. Stack (1996:2) introduces "Miss Pearl," and sets the stage for her discussion of the sentiments, stresses, ideals, and practicalities that influence return migration with these words:

> Maybe it was never much of a house, but after all these years its tin roof has buckled and gapped, and the framing has pulled back from the window sills, leaving cracks big enough for cats. Pearl's blankets shade the windows. But the number of children over the years who came to call this house home, and to call Pearl Bishop "Miss Pearl," is almost beyond counting: there were Pearl and Samuel's own ten, and all the nieces and nephews sent back and forth by parents in New York, and there were the two little cousins who came after their mother passed—fourteen children at least at many a time, and sometimes seventeen, sometimes more. There are still children in the house, grandchildren now. Pearl is still Miss Pearl.

Stack (1996) illuminates throughout her book that in spite of the material conditions that, from a middle-class suburban perspective, are lacking, Miss Pearl and others successfully care for and bring up several children. The networks of care among individuals and families of these rural counties of Mississippi, South Carolina, and North Carolina show that allowing children to circulate among families may be a consciously chosen way of reinforcing certain social, cultural, emotional, and political-economic relationships but may also be one informal practice among many used in times of need as families struggle to support themselves.

Transracial Adoption: Issues and Debates

Although the movie *Secrets and Lies* met with critical acclaim, it is not primarily about adoption or race in the end. The film raises the questions of what it means to be related by birth, but Leigh's concern is with the dynamics of relationships, with what we keep from or share with the other people in our lives. The larger racial and class politics of adoption in London or elsewhere barely reach the surface, even as the racial, gender, and class identities of the characters serve as a foil to assumptions about the affective closeness and conventional conviviality of families. As adoption has become less stigmatized during the second half of the twentieth century, public discussion and even debate about interracial adoption has become more prevalent.

As Rothman notes, interracial adoption brings to light the "hard nut of race" (Rothman 2005:88–89). Transracial adoption assumes that there are races for a child to move between. The most discussed statement on transracial adoption was made in 1972 by the National Association of Black Social Workers (NABSW), which called for the end of adoptions of black children by white parents. The NABSW argued for

> the inviolable position of black children in black families where they belong physically, psychologically and culturally in order that they receive the total sense of themselves and develop a sound projection of their future. . . . We know there are numerous alternatives to the placement of black children with white families and challenge all agencies and organizations to commit themselves to the basic concept of black families for black children. (Adoption History Project, http://darkwing.uoregon.edu/~adoption/)

The NABSW and others have argued that these issues around transracial adoption need attention because we live in a racist society. In such an environment, ignoring the politics and power of race is also problematic. "While 'colorblindness' has frequently been embraced as antiracist, it has also been shown to be an evasion of race that situates Whiteness as the 'norm' and denies the salience of racial difference" (Frankenberg 1993, cited in Patton 2000:49).

The problem that social workers raised in the 1970s is that white parents will not understand the problem of race. They will not understand the "totality of the problem of being black in this society," states Edmund D. Jones, assistant director of family and children's services in Baltimore, in a 1972 article (cited in Patton 2000:49–50). From this perspective,

> love was an insufficient condition for constructive growth.... Transracial adoptions made the disastrous mistake of imagining that racial identity was something black children, surrounded by white relatives, could achieve all by themselves. They could not. Individualistic conceptions of how children grew up were luxuries associated with majority group membership, not accurate descriptions of the hurdles that black children faced in a racist society. Without same-race parents, black children would be left defenseless against bigotry; they would need "to be taught to do what comes naturally." Instead of promoting their interests, transracial adoption made children even more vulnerable victims of racism. (Herman 2008:249)

Although the overt exclusion of black babies from the adoption process had been at least partly ameliorated in the 1970s, the distinction between racial groups was considered self-evident, and racial discrimination remained embedded in social and political-economic institutions.

In the twenty-first-century United States, the NABSW statement continues to challenge people to recognize the racial and ethnic discrimination that is a fact of life for African Americans and other racial and ethnic groups and the necessity for children to learn from their families how to navigate this discrimination. Legal scholar Patricia Williams points to the implicit racial sentiments when she asks,

> Is there not something unseemly, in our society, about the spectacle of a white woman mothering a black child? A white woman giving totally to a black child; a black child totally and demandingly dependent for everything, sustenance itself, from a white woman. . . . The utter interdependence of such an image, the merging it implies; the giving up of boundary; the encompassing of other within self; the unbounded generosity and interconnectedness of such an image. . . . (Williams 1991:226, quoted in Rothman 2005:95)

Without question, adopting parents and adopted children break down assumed boundaries through their love and care for each other. Nevertheless, black adopted children and white adopting parents confront the questions of racial and ethnic identity, racism, and how to defend oneself against discrimination. In recent years, individuals who were adopted as children, sometimes across commonly recognized racial boundaries, have begun to contribute to public discourse about adoption, identity, discrimination, and the best interests of children (e.g., Trenka, Oparah, and Shin 2006).

Through the idiom of hair, some adopted black children (and their white adopting parents) have learned about these complex issues. Adoptee Jeni Wright, who identifies as biracial, writes that her parents had always told her that "love is colorblind" (Wright 2006:28). She remembers that by the time she was in first grade she realized the limits of that ideal when a "little girl stands in the aisle of the school bus and declares that she cannot sit next to me because of my skin color" (Wright 2006:28). She was 12 when her parents adopted a second child, also a biracial girl, and she vowed that her sister would "not suffer the way I had. At the very least they would learn how to do her hair" (Wright 2006:28). Her short essay expresses her profound anger and frustration when on her first visit home from college she discovered that her sister's long curls had turned into matted dreadlocks because her mother did not take the time to properly comb her sister's hair.

From a different perspective, Barbara Katz Rothman writes about how hair reflects the larger racial issues involved in adoption and U.S. society more generally. Rothman, a white mother who adopted a black child, wanted to let her daughter's hair be wild, be natural. But through the exhortations of her black friends, Rothman (2005:217) came to a very different understanding of hair.

> And that's the conundrum: the little soft baby Afro, the wild young-girl hair, is intended by the white mother as a celebration of difference. It ends up being a disregarding of culture. A culture has developed—out of the experience of the hair itself, out of a response to racial denigration, and also out of self-love and pride and joy—that tells people how to deal with that hair. And loose, unbound, wild—that's not it.

Thus, white parents may be trying to teach their adopted black children to love themselves by allowing them to have natural hair. "But they're not teaching their kids how to be black in America" (Rothman 2005:217).

Although even in the 1990s, scholars such as Bartholet (1999) decried any attempt to limit the adoption of black children by whites, few recognize the ways in which race matching occurs all the time. In other words, if adoption truly were color-blind, if people could not choose the racial or gendered category to which their child belongs, then a black couple would be just as likely to adopt a white infant as a white couple. The high demand for white infants by white couples and the economics of the adoption process make the generalized adoption of white infants by black, Latino, or Asian families simply a thought experiment, as Hawley Fogg-Davis (2002) points out in *The Ethics of Transracial Adoption*. In other words, adoption across racial boundaries is often a privilege of white women and men. The racial and class politics of adopting children is not new, although it has been configured in new ways in recent decades. For example, in 1940,

> a group of 40 New York Irish orphans was sent to live with Catholic families in Arizona. However, the Catholics turned out to be Mexican Americans, and the local Anglos were so outraged at this transgression of race boundaries that they instigated a mass abduction of the children, carried out at gunpoint. (Hübinette 2006:141)

The Arizona Anglos were more concerned with maintaining a racial boundary between themselves and Mexican Americans, whereas on the east coast, the Irish were despised as a separate race, not white at all. "Through this direct action, transracial adoption as a white privilege was resolutely reinstated, and this privilege continues in the contemporary era" (Hübinette 2006:141). The NABSW statement on transracial adoption is, and was, controversial in part because it challenges this privilege at the same that it redraws essentialized racial categories.

From a different perspective, and as we will discuss in more detail in the next chapter, transnational adoption also helps us to understand the role of race in adoption. While many (not all) such adoptions are across racial boundaries, the term *transracial* is rarely used to describe them. That rhetorical move can be partly attributed to the ways that the category Asian has been used in the United States in ways very different from African American or black. Asians and Asian Americans have been on the one hand feared and vilified, the subject of campaigns against a "yellow peril" (Lee 1999), and restricted from basic rights of citizenship—even long after African Americans were granted them. On the other hand, Asians are depicted as a model minority, in ways that implicitly compare the success of (some) Asians to the failures of (some) blacks.

White adopting parents will sometimes speak about how much "easier" it is to adopt and raise an Asian child than a black child in the United States today, thereby obscuring the possible racial or ethnic discrimination an Asian child may face and avoiding confrontation with issues of race more generally (Kim 2008). One such adopting parent explains to scholar Sara Dorow (2006b:47),

> To be honest, with me it was a racial thing. I didn't want a black child, and it was pretty much China or South America and in South America you could get kids of color, and I didn't want to do that. . . . And I just don't have any biases about Asians, so for me it was an easier fit. . . . I mean black is still, uh, not only a minority to me in this country, but a minority that doesn't fit in, as well as some other minorities.

When potential adoptive parents who are white request a white infant, or a child who is perceived to fit in more easily, the practice is not considered racial matching and does not draw the negative reactions that NABSW did when it argued that black parents should be the only families adopting black infants. The absence of attention to the regular race matching that does go on when white parents adopt white children underscores how it is nonwhite categories of race—here, black—that get marked as asking for special consideration.

As Briggs (2003) points out, the NABSW statement must be understood in the context of political and social relationships of the 1970s. The Civil Rights Act had finally been passed in 1964, outlawing racial segregation. Although whites adopting American Indian or African American children might have seen their efforts as supporting racial integration, African American communities recognized that children who looked black needed the resources of the African American community to learn how to deal with the entrenched racism they would inevitably encounter. Many white Americans had little or no exposure to African American social relations, culture, language, or history, much less the economic and political discrimination that blacks faced. Just loving a child was not enough. Although the position of black social workers has softened since that 1972 statement, they still encourage supporting adoption within the African American community. Just as important, some members of the African American community have recognized and spoken out about the ways that pervasive stereotypes about black mothers and black families make it easier for the state to remove children from their families rather than help the families better support their children.

The Foster System and Adoption in the United States

Assumptions about race are often embedded in discussions of fostering and adoption in ways that all but obscure the state's uneven intervention into the lives of certain families, into the choices women and men make as they navigate the social and political-economic terrain of parenting. Based on extensive research of public documents and statistics, Dorothy Roberts (2002) demonstrates the continuing struggle of the African American community to resist state intervention into their families. Integrating discussion of fostering and adoption with child welfare at the turn of the twenty-first century, Roberts shows that while white families who are struggling financially are offered other options, black families are more likely to have had their children taken away from them. Black children are overrepresented in the national foster care population (Roberts 2002:8). Nationwide, African American children constitute about 17 percent of the general population but 42 percent of the foster population. The problem is more evident in larger cities. Roberts (2002:8–9) offers San Francisco and New York City as examples: In San Francisco in 1994, approximately 10 percent of the city's population was black, but 70 percent of the foster population was black. Across the country in New York City, the foster population in 1997 was 73 percent black, 3 percent white, and less than 24 percent Latino. At the end of the twentieth century, 1 out of every 22 black children in New York City was in foster care; in some neighborhoods, such as Central Harlem, 1 out of 10 children was in foster care. For white children, the odds were better, with only 1 out of 385 in foster care (Roberts 2002:9).

In areas where blacks are more of a minority, the overrepresentation of black children in foster care is even greater. Thus, in places such as Minnesota or Maine, where the census counts less than 2 percent of the population as black, the chances that these children will be placed in foster care skyrockets to 15 times their proportion of the population (Roberts 2002:9–10). In contrast, Latino and Asian American children are underrepresented in fostered populations. Although the absolute numbers of children in the foster population have surely changed in the years since Roberts published *Shattered Bonds*, the patterning of statistics that Roberts lays out is sobering.

The overrepresentation of some groups in foster care reflects the linkage of race and socioeconomic class in the United States as well as the ways that categories, such as neglect, may be interpreted by social workers and courts. In the United States, people generally understand fostering in terms of the state-controlled system of foster care, in which social workers and judges intervene to remove children from their families or immediate caregivers, place them in certified foster homes or institutional settings, and determine the conditions under which children may, or may not, eventually return to parents or relatives. According to Duncan Lindsey, "inadequacy of income, *more than any factor,* constitutes the reason that children are removed" (cited in Roberts 2002:35). The category of neglect is "intended to capture only incidents where parents have the ability to provide for their children and fail to do so, [but] neglect is usually hard to disentangle from poverty" (Roberts 2002:34). And as is evident from Roberts's (2002) study, race is both tied up with and erased from the removal of children from their families.

The problematic definition of neglect is clear in a case that moved from local San Diego court to the Supreme Court in 1969, as Solinger (2001:184) describes. Kathleen Ramos, a member of the Rinion Band of Mission Indians, was made a ward of the court because she was truant from high school. The teenager had missed four days or more of school in a two-week period. The hearing took place in the Juvenile Department of the Superior Court of California, County of San Diego, and 15-year-old Kathy and her mother, Marcella Mason, could not afford a lawyer, had not been provided a lawyer at the expense of the county, and had not been given written notice about the nature of the proceedings or their rights. After that hearing Kathy was removed from her mother's care and placed with her grandparents. Kathy was required to attend summer school but again missed several days because of chronic bronchitis and difficulty in traveling to her school, which was four miles away. The family could not afford a vehicle.

In 1969, the case was pursued up to the U.S. Supreme Court because of its generalizability to other cases in which children who were removed from poor families were transferred to economically more stable families who would then receive a subsidy for foster care. At the hearing the school district's representative, a Mrs. Cavey, had said that Kathy "should be put in a home where there was a car which could get her where she wants to go" (Solinger 2001:184). Solinger writes, "When Kathy's lawyers tried to prevent the state from removing the girl from her family, they pointed to Mrs. Cavey's dictum as a 'firm indication that, indeed, the poverty of Kathy's family is to blame for her troubles'" (Solinger 2001:184). At that time, foster parents would receive a grant of $105 a month to take care of a child whose mother might receive only one third that amount in support (Solinger 2001:185). Such funding, if given to a birth parent like Kathy's mother, might allow her to buy a necessity such as a car.

We have seen that when birth parents are not able to care for children (or when people place a particular cultural value on fosterage), individuals and communities may step in to care for children informally. However difficult the decision to allow a relative or friend to care for one's own child may be, it is quite another thing to have a child removed from one's household against one's will. In many communities, especially white and wealthier communities, individuals may know little about foster care and may never have encountered child protective services. However, as Roberts (2002:75) points out, "most people in poor minority neighborhoods have either had a terrifying encounter with child protective services or know someone who has. They have a legitimate fear that it might happen to them. . . . The child welfare system has a powerful, menacing presence in these communities." It is predominantly the children of African American and poor families and communities who are the most likely to be removed from their homes and the people who care for them. A home like that of Miss Pearl most likely would not have been registered as a foster home because of its material condition, and in fact, a social worker might have removed children if he or she had seen the lack of resources as a kind of neglect.

Roberts (2002) and others (e.g., Briggs 2003; Solinger 2001) convincingly show that welfare and other support systems that enable poor parents to nurture and raise their children have been systematically removed since the mid-1990s. Simultaneously, tax credits and supplements have been made available to white middle-class parents to adopt these same children. Although racial politics have shifted to a more inclusive stance, as Laura Briggs (2006b:85) notes, "poverty rates for those who understood themselves as Latinos, American Indians, Alaskan Natives, and African Americans remained more than three times the rate for whites, while for Asians and Pacific Islanders it remained one and a half times higher." Moreover, the 1980s and 1990s saw welfare reform and new adoption legislation that further eroded the support offered to poor families to support birth children, even as it made adoption for the middle class easier.

As Briggs (2006b:84–85) points out,

> even as welfare reform all but eliminated federal transfer payments to help working-class women raise their own children, the 1996 adoption reform provided a $6000 tax break to (implicitly white) middle-class families who adopted "special needs" children—with nonwhite as subcategory of the definition of special needs. Combined with the 1980 federal Adoption Assistance and Child Welfare Act that provided subsidies to middle- and upper-class families adopting from foster care, the adoption tax credit meant that the federal government would provide upwards of a $13,000 bonus for middle-class white people to raise the same children taken from families for poverty-related neglect that it wouldn't pay to alleviate.

Thus, it is not strictly race or socioeconomic class but rather the way class and race intersect in the United States that has resulted in the number of African American children removed from their homes and placed into foster care, often with little chance for a stable home.

Meanwhile, downstream of these decisions to remove children from their parents, the foster system in the United States struggles to find both foster homes for children and permanent homes for children. In 2007, 51,000 children were adopted from the foster care system, but there were 130,000 other children waiting to be adopted (http://www.acf.hhs.gov/programs/cb/stats_research/afcars/trends.htm). Many states and even private agencies have used a variety of techniques and forms of communication to try to enlist families to help with these children. Websites contain pages of photos of "waiting children," and some agencies put up displays at malls or other public places, all with the hope that such publicity will result in more families' stepping forward to adopt children. Rey, 14 years old, has been in foster care for 11 years; in that time, he has lived with seven families. He and an adoption placement service, Heart Gallery NYC, are hoping that the use of marketing strategies to find families—putting photos and information about children hoping to be adopted in places such as libraries and airports—will help him and other children like him to find families. "I'll do what I got to do to get a family," Rey says (Barry 2007). With these new methods of finding homes for children, some children will be more likely to be adopted into "forever families." But many of these children will remain in foster care—often moving from one foster family to another—for their entire childhood.

Native Americans and Adoption in the United States and Canada

The ways state intervention into families through child protection and welfare policies is tied to racial politics becomes clearer with comparison to the explicit policies of the United States and Canada to remove aboriginal or native children from their families. Accounting for less than 1 percent of the population of the United States, American Indians are often classified as a minority. However, Native Americans are, as Stark and Stark (2006:126) point out, in a unique position because they have a "government-to-government relationship, formalized through treaty making." By the 1880s, the U.S. government acknowledged that Congress, not individual state governments, was the body responsible for dealing with Indian nations. In that decade as well, the United States "first imposed a federal boarding school policy intended to force American Indians to assimilate into American society, rather than segregating them by removing them from their lands and confining them on reservations" (Stark and Stark 2006:126). In the United States many of these schools closed by the mid-1920s. By the 1940s, a growing belief that institutional living was detrimental to children increased the push to have native children adopted into nonnative families (Stark and Stark 2006:127). Boarding schools intended to "civilize" native children were also popular in Canada. When residential schools in Canada closed in the 1960s, "over 11,000 children were removed from their communities" (Snow and Covell 2006:109–10) and adopted into nonnative families in what is widely known as the "sixties scoop."

Like African American children in the 1990s, Native American children in the 1960s and 1970s were adopted at rates much high than those of other children. First, there was a high chance they would end up in foster care. "In Wisconsin, the likelihood of Native American children being removed from their families was 1,600 percent greater than that of non-native Americans" (Simon and Hernandez 2008:1). And when placed into adopting homes, they were likely to be placed transracially: In 1969, 89 percent of Native American children in foster care ended up being placed with families of a different racial group. By 1978 between 25 and 35 percent of all Indian children were separated from their families and placed in foster homes, adoptive homes, or institutions (Brown and Rieger 2001:60–61; Stark and Stark 2006:131). Although the adoption of American Indian and aboriginal Canadian children into families cannot be understood as having the same consequences as requiring students to attend boarding school, many scholars and activists point to the long history of the removal of children and the overall impact on communities as well as individuals. Over the course of several decades, from the late nineteenth century up until the mid-1990s, perhaps 50,000 children were removed from aboriginal families in the United States and Canada; in Australia, approximately 25,000 aboriginal children were removed to boarding schools and foster care between 1900 and 1970 (Hübinette 2006:141). As Roberts (2002) notes, removing a child is perhaps the most traumatic of state interventions, having a lasting impact on children, their families, and the community. Moreover, the arguments used by state agencies that Native American families were less capable of raising their children—and thus the removal was in the best interest of the children (Stark and Stark 2006:131)—are similar to those used to remove children from families today.

In spite of the high rates at which Native American children were removed from their homes in the 1960s and 1970s, there is little research on the adoption and fostering of Native American children in the United States. In 1958, the Bureau of Indian Affairs and the Child Welfare League of America established the Indian Adoption Project to promote "external placement" of American Indian children. This program placed approximately 395 children with white families over the course of nine years. For five years between 1958 and 1967, David Fanshel followed 97 of these American Indian children who were adopted into non-Indian homes, mostly in states distant from their reservations, in an attempt to understand whether and how they adjusted. One of the most important findings of the study described in *Far From the Reservation* (Fanshel 1972) was that the age of the child affected his or her adjustment, with older children having more difficulty integrating into their new families and communities. The social status of parents also played a role in adoptees' adjustment, with higher social status of adoptive parents linked to an adoptee's greater difficulty in adjusting. The study was based on adoptive parents' reports of behavior and perceptions of child's adjustment, not on what children said. The study also showed a complex and complicated set of views about adoption and race among parents—and different degrees of ability or interest in raising a "transracial adopted" child.

More recently, adult Native Americans who were adopted as children have spoken out about their experiences and struggles to belong to white communities and families (e.g., Simon and Hernandez 2008; Trenka et al. 2006). In their interviews with adult Native Americans who were adopted into white families, Simon and Hernandez (2008) find that many adoptees, even when their adopting parents treated them with love and respect, often were separated from Native American culture. Andrea, adopted by white parents, explains about how her adoptive parents addressed her Native American background:

> My parents never really said, you're American Indian and that is something to be very much proud of. . . . So I had to go through all that stuff, I guess, on my own. That made it really difficult growing up. Because I didn't know if I should be proud of it or if I should be embarrassed about it. . . . I basically grew up white and I had no Indian heritage until I got older and I started doing my own research and reading. (Simon and Hernandez 2008:36–37)

And although Andrea feels that her adoptive parents were very good to her, as an adult, she came to believe that Indian children should not be placed in white adoptive families. She says, "I love my family, don't get me wrong . . . but I think growing up probably wouldn't have been so hard if I would have grown up with my own heritage" (Simon and Hernandez 2008:42).

Additionally, several scholars argue that the displacement of children from their families caused problems for individuals and "weakened Native communities" (Brown and Rieger 2001:60–61; also see Mills and Champion 1996; Simon and Hernandez 2008). The removal of children from American Indian communities along with the growing political activism around issues of citizenship, autonomy, education, economic and political disenfranchisement, and discrimination set the stage for landmark legislation first introduced in 1972 and passed in 1978. The Indian Child Welfare Act (ICWA) was "designed to prevent the decimation of Indian tribes and the breakdown of Indian families by the transracial placement of Native American children . . . [and] to safeguard Native American culture by keeping families and tribes together and within their native environment" (Simon and Hernandez 2008:1). Congress recognized that many social workers at the time were judging Indian homes according to white middle-class standards. More important, they were obscuring the history of racial thinking and action that denied Native Americans their rights, lands, autonomy, and values, exacerbating the lack of economic viability of communities. The act also reinforced the special status of Native American tribes because prior to the ICWA, "Congress found that the states often failed to recognize the 'essential tribal relations of Indian people and the cultural and social standard prevailing in Indian communities and families'" (Brown and Rieger 2001:60–61). Over the past four decades, subsequent court decisions have emphasized that courts must take account of the best interests of the particular tribe into which a child is born as well as the best interests of the child (Simon and Hernandez 2008:5). The laws also make explicit the preference for a child to be placed with a member of the child's extended family, a member of the child's tribe, or another Indian family (Simon and Hernandez 2008:2).

Implementing the ICWA and other native child welfare legislation is, however, often complicated, requiring a delicate balance between conflicting state and federal laws, social workers and child protective services, tribal communities, families, and children themselves. Toward this end, the law requires state courts to use higher standards of proof in removing native children from their homes under state authority ("serious imminent physical damage or harm" in contrast to "contrary to the welfare of the child"), places a higher burden on state agencies to provide services ("active" efforts in contrast to "reasonable" efforts), and explicitly provides for the consideration of the cultural background of the child. Further, ICWA recognizes the rights of tribes to intervene in state proceedings (Brown and Rieger 2001:61).

In a discussion of the kinds of placement dilemmas that arise, Brown and Rieger (2001:66) relate the story of a child who was part Native American and part African American and was placed in a foster home where the foster mother was Eskimo (probably Inupiaq or Yup'ik). Although an African American aunt living in another state had the resources and desire to foster and later adopt the child, "the village that intervened on behalf of the child was adamantly opposed to the placement, citing that it would remove the child from a Native environment and outside of Alaska." Although the Department of Family and Youth Services preferred to place the child with a "blood relative," the village made the native foster family the first preference both so that the child would not have to bond to another family and so that the child would remain linked to the community. This example illustrates that the "best interests" of the child require consideration not just of the child's lifespan but of the welfare of the "whole circle," from great-great-grandparents of the child to the child's future children and grandchildren, addressing the community's notions of place and time (Brown and Rieger 2001:67). The example also illustrates the ways in which Native American identity and culture may be essentialized and claimed differently than African American identity and culture.

To a large extent, understanding the deep connections between the child and the tribe leads in a direction opposite that established by most child welfare decisions. In most child welfare cases, a larger group is not identified or seen to be affected by the child's welfare; the preceding examples raise the possibility that the welfare of the group relies on the welfare of the child (Brown and Rieger 2001:65). Although no single law like ICWA exists in Canada, as a way to "compensate for historical wrongs against Aboriginal families and children," Canada has expressed concern with Article 21 of the UN Convention on the Rights of the Child, which calls for the "state regulation of adoption." By raising questions about Article 21, the Canadian government recognizes "aboriginal control over the adoption of aboriginal children" (Snow and Covell 2006:109). The government complaint underscores the ways that redresses to past action against native families may operate differently than rules for removing children from, for example, African American homes and communities.

Conclusions

In the United States during the second half of the twentieth century, the stream of discourse about the naturalness of birth and the importance of birth parents caring for children in the creation of families collided with a stream of discourse about the best interests of children and a set of economic and political institutions that disregarded or overrode assumptions about the significance of birth. Forefronting the state institution of fostering in the United States brings to light the ways some parents are assumed to be better than others; it also raises the issue of who should be parenting and how the state or the community attempts to protect children.

As Roberts (2002:2478) points out, what "appeared radical to many Americans in the NABSW's resolution was echoed in United Nations protections of endangered cultures" and in the ICWA—that transmission of cultural knowledge to children is crucial to the maintenance of cultures and communities. Some Native American/First Nations tribes in northwest British Columbia, for example, see individuals as the reincarnations of returned family members (Mills and Champion 1996). ICWA provides some local control and a different model of constituting families. The formal and informal kinship practices, religious beliefs, narrative traditions, and symbolic resources of African American communities are not recognized by law or taken into account in institutional discussions about raising children.

As we argue in Chapter 3, what is crucial in the state's interventions in families is the way U.S. society understands where the responsibility for children lies and the economics of that belief. The underlying philosophy of the child welfare system is, as Roberts (2002) notes, based on the presumption that children's basic needs for sustenance and development must and can be met solely by parents. The state intervenes to provide special institutionalized services—primarily placing children in foster care—only when parents fail to fulfill their child-rearing obligations. The child protection approach is inextricably tied to our society's refusal to see a collective responsibility for children's welfare. It is a society that is willing to pay billions of dollars a year to maintain poor children outside their homes but begrudges spending a fraction of that to support families and enable children to stay with their birth parents (Roberts 2002:89). Countries such as Norway respond quite differently; government support for all families in Norway has made forcible removal of a child from a family a rare event. Native American communities approach relationships between child and community differently still, placing priority on maintaining or enhancing cultural, tribal, and community relationships.

In an era when many white Americans would deny that overt racism persists, the claim that the foster and child welfare system is overtly racist and operates to maintain racial boundaries must be carefully examined. Particularly important are the ways that race and socioeconomic status are so intertwined. Thus, determining whether race or socioeconomic class is the cause of the overrepresentation of African American children who are removed from their families is difficult. Families of color are overrepresented among the poor. Based on figures from 1980 through the 1990s, the percentage of black children who ever lived in poverty while growing up is about the same as the percentage of white children who have never lived in poverty (Roberts 2002:47). Yet even when socioeconomic status is controlled, blacks are still overrepresented in foster care. Racial bias is evident within the child protection system at multiple levels and at various points in institutional procedures—including when infants are taken from their mothers (e.g., at birth if mothers are tested because of suspicion of drug use), how long children are in foster care, how long it takes to reunite children and families, under which kinds of plans children are reunited with families, and the extent to which services to aid reunification are available. Even when they have the same problems and characteristics as white children, black children are more likely to be removed from their parents (Roberts 2002:17).

By considering the fostering and adoption of American Indian and African American children, we expand our understanding of the ways that the state controls the private lives of citizens and has engaged in constituting racial boundaries through adoption. The presumed naturalness of birth parents' caring for, raising, and remaining emotionally, socially, and economically connected to their children unravels when positioned against the racial and class-based assumptions about the needs of a child or the fitness of the mother. Even though social workers long believed that maintaining birth families intact was best, this approach was not enacted in all cases; it has not always been a priority of social workers, state governments, or local governments to maintain the biological relationship of parent and child by supporting poor and minority families. Roberts (2002:17–18) begs her readers to recognize that removing children "from their homes is perhaps the most severe government intrusion into the lives of citizens. It is also one of the most terrifying experiences a child can have."

Many individuals in the United States assume that the birth parents are the best people to care for a child. Our attention to fostering in west African and Pacific societies in Chapter 1 demonstrates the ways in which the naturalness of parenting may be configured differently in different societies. In other words, in some societies, fostering is more natural than raising a biological child. In west African and Andean communities, children are fostered in homes, not forcibly removed against the family's wishes. Children may know both sets of parents or make their own decisions about whether to move. At the same time, even in societies in which fostering is widespread, children often move from households with fewer resources to those with more resources. Similarly, although families are presumed to be founded on genealogical or biological ties, many people in the United States would recognize unrelated individuals as part of the family because of the close relationships developed through the sharing of food, talk, children, commodities, and experiences. What an examination of the politics of race makes clear is that even as adoption appears to be an individual decision, it is deeply rooted in the politics, norms, and institutions of any society.

5

The Practices of
Transnational Adoption

In this chapter, we examine transnational adoption. We choose to use the term *transnational* rather than *international* or *intercountry* to describe these adoptions because doing so signals the importance of the ways that the flow of children from sending to receiving countries—like the flow of other people, things, capital, or ideas—mirrors pathways of power, authority, and inequality, this time on a global scale. Thus, while such movement of goods, ideas, and people is not unidirectional, it is true that some things and certain kinds of people are more likely to move in one direction rather than another (Riley 1997). In addition, *transnational* signals a more complex process than *international;* transnational adoptions are best understood as the result of complex and sometimes contradictory processes at all levels—local, national, and global.

We begin this chapter by looking at the patterns of transnational adoption and asking what we can learn from the numbers, timing, and direction of adoptions. From these patterns, it is clear that the pathways along which children travel across borders have been and continue to be shaped by relations and historical events both within sending and receiving countries and between countries. As we will show, even the international agreements that govern the movement of children around adoption reflect these patterns of influence and inequality.

Transnational history, patterns, and connections also affect the experience of adoptees once they settle in their new homes and communities. For example, whereas once adoptees did not usually have ties to their countries of birth, the increasing contacts with and information about all parts of the world have served to make continuing contact between adoptees and their home countries both possible and even expected. In addition, and sometimes connected to those changes, the growing importance of issues of identity and identity politics in the United States and in other countries has certainly had an influence on the ways that adoptees and their families see adoption and issues of race, ethnicity, and nationality.

Moreover, the changes within sending and receiving countries have also played roles in the shifting patterns of transnational adoption. South Korea's economic and political changes and its increasing wealth and global influence, for example, have played a significant role in the decline of adoptions out of that country. As we discuss in more detail below, Korea's growing world clout allowed, and even inspired, it to attempt to limit its role as a sending country. India too has tried to limit international adoptions; its relatively restrictive policies concerning foreign adoption may be related to India's colonial experience and the ways that, partly as a reaction to that colonial past, it has attempted to develop an "alternative modernity" (Appadurai 1991). On the other hand, the recent increase of transnational adoptions out of Ethiopia (Selman 2006), especially in the past 10 years, may be partly attributable to how Ethiopia is now part of the global consciousness in a way it was not in the past. Here, it is as much outside attention and interest in the plight of orphaned children as domestic initiative that has been behind the increases in the adoption of Ethiopian children by foreigners (particularly Europeans).

One of the first questions to raise is why anyone, in fact many people, turn to other countries to adopt children. The answer to this question is not a simple one. As we will discuss below, early adoptions from European countries and those from Asia to Western countries were seen as humanitarian gestures, coming after crises of war or severe poverty in the sending countries. Increased contact with and information about all parts of the world has meant that people around the world hear easily and quickly about events taking place in other parts of the world; in that way, the rise in the migration of children for adoption mirrors the rise in migrations of people for many other reasons. But all transnational adoptions, even those that are reactions to crises in sending countries, are patterned after involvement between countries and reflect understandings and ideologies deeply rooted in sending and receiving countries. In more recent years, as the numbers of available infants—particularly white healthy infants—have declined in most Western countries, adoption from other societies is seen as an acceptable alternative. Some even see such adoptions as preferred, partly because the parents of these children are often unknown and untraceable. This, some parents feel, will make the adoption "cleaner," with little danger of a birth mother's coming to reclaim her child years later.

Ana Ortiz and Laura Briggs (2003) offer an alternative reason for Americans' turning to adopting overseas even as there were children available for adoption through the American foster system. They argue that media and public policies combined in the 1990s to make poor families in the United States—and thus the children of these poor families—seem pathological and thus unredeemable and undesirable as potential adoptees. These authors argue that the poor have come to be seen "as a biological underclass" (2003: 53). At the same time, the poor children of other countries were constructed as "savable"; in this characterization, adopting these children had a potential successful outcome that adoption of poor American children could not.

The Global Transfer of Children

In 2000, some 40,000 children were adopted by foreigners across the world. While many countries participate in international adoption, most of the adopted children end up in relatively few countries. The United States has the highest number of international adoptions; in fact, the United States accounts for more intercountry adoptions than the next 13 countries combined (Menozzi 2008); in 2007, nearly 20,000 children were adopted from other countries by U.S. citizens (http://www.travel.state.gov/family/adoption/stats/stats_451.html) (see Figure 5.1). Other countries, such as France and

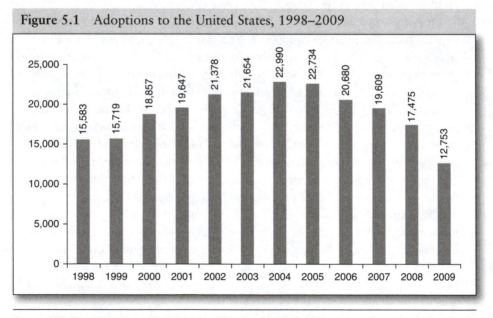

Figure 5.1   Adoptions to the United States, 1998–2009

Source: U.S. State Department, Intercountry Adoption (http://adoption.state.gov/news/total_chart.html).

Spain, also adopt many children internationally. But there are some countries, such as Norway, that adopt fewer children internationally (438 children in 2006) (Statistics Norway, http://www.ssb.no/adopsjon_en/) but who nevertheless have high rates of adoption per capita. In these countries, with their smaller populations, transnational adoptions can have large impacts on the general society.

The sending countries with the largest numbers of children being adopted by foreigners are China, Guatemala, South Korea, the Russian Federation, and the Ukraine (Menozzi 2008). But these numbers have changed over the past couple decades. Most notably, the number of adoptions from Korea, once the largest sending country, has declined. The number from China has steadily increased since the government first formally opened up the adoption of Chinese children to foreigners. Relatively few children are adopted internationally from Africa or the Caribbean (see Table 5.1).

From the information in Table 5.2, we can clearly see that children involved in adoption move from the global South to the global North, from

Table 5.1 International adoptions: Top 20 sending countries, United States, 2004–2009

	Fiscal Year					
Rank	2009	2008	2007	2006	2005	2004
1	China	Guatemala	China	China	China	China
	3,001	4,122	5,423	6,492	7,903	7,044
2	Ethiopia	China	Guatemala	Guatemala	Russia	Russia
	2,277	3,911	4,727	4,135	4,631	5,865
3	Russia	Russia	Russia	Russia	Guatemala	Guatemala
	1,586	1,857	2,303	3,702	3,783	3,264
4	South Korea	Ethiopia	Ethiopia	South Korea	South Korea	South Korea
	1,080	1,724	1,254	1,373	1,628	1,716
5	Guatemala	South Korea	South Korea	Ethiopia	Ukraine	Kazakhstan
	756	1,065	938	731	824	826
6	Ukraine	Vietnam	Vietnam	Kazakhstan	Kazakhstan	Ukraine
	610	748	828	588	755	723

(Continued)

Table 5.1 (Continued)

Rank	Fiscal Year					
	2009	2008	2007	2006	2005	2004
7	Vietnam	Ukraine	Ukraine	Ukraine	Ethiopia	India
	481	490	613	463	442	406
8	Haiti	Kazakhstan	Kazakhstan	Liberia	India	Haiti
	330	380	547	353	323	356
9	India	India	India	Colombia	Colombia	Ethiopia
	297	308	411	344	287	289
10	Kazakhstan	Colombia	Liberia	India	Philippines	Colombia
	295	306	314	319	268	287
11	Philippines	Haiti	Colombia	Haiti	Haiti	Belarus
	281	310	309	310	234	202
12	Taiwan	Philippines	Philippines	Philippines	Liberia	Philippines
	253	2392	260	248	183	196
13	Colombia	Liberia	Haiti	Taiwan	Taiwan	Bulgaria
	238	254	191	187	141	110
14	Nigeria	Taiwan	Taiwan	Vietnam	Mexico	Poland
	110	219	184	163	88	102
15	Ghana	Nigeria	Mexico	Mexico	Poland	Mexico
	103	149	89	70	73	89
16	Mexico	Mexico	Poland	Poland	Thailand	Liberia
	72	105	84	67	71	86
17	Uganda	Ghana	Thailand	Nepal	Brazil	Nepal
	69	97	66	66	66	73
18	Thailand	Kyrgyzstan	Brazil	Brazil	Nigeria	Nigeria
	56	78	65	66	65	71
19	Jamaica	Poland	Kyrgyzstan	Nigeria	Jamaica	Brazil
	54	77	54	62	62	69
20	Poland	Thailand	Uganda	Thailand	Nepal	Thailand
	50	59	54	56	62	69

Source: U.S. State Department, Intercountry Adoption (http://adoption.state.gov/news/total_chart.html).

poor to rich countries. Whereas per capita income for the top five receiving countries is nearly $17,000 and over (the United States has a per capital income of over $37,000), the sending countries are much poorer, with most having per capital incomes well under $5,000 (see Figure 5.2).

Table 5.2   Per capita income of major sending and receiving countries, 2003

Country	Number of Adoptions	Per Capita Income (US$)
Sending countries		
China	11,230	1,100
Russia	7,659	2,610
Guatemala	2,673	1,910
Korea	2,306	12,030
Ukraine	1,958	970
Colombia	1,750	1,810
India	1,172	530
Haiti	1,055	380
Bulgaria	962	2,130
Vietnam	935	480
Receiving countries		
United States	21,616	37,610
France	3,995	24,770
Spain	3,951	16,990
Italy	2,772	21,560
Canada	2,180	23,930

Source: Selman (2006, Tables 12 and 13).

Rules Governing Intercountry Adoptions

Not only do the patterns of movement of children between countries follow historical experience, structures of influence and power, and local ideology, but even the agreements between countries reflect some of these same influences. The most recent and influential regulation governing transnational adoptions is the Hague Convention on the Protection of Children and

Cooperation in Respect of Intercountry Adoption (usually referred to as "the Hague Convention"); it was first enacted in 1993 and has been ratified by different countries across the globe since then. This act makes the best interests of the child paramount. Indeed, it aims to protect children from exploitation and harm. At the same time, the conventions and assumptions it outlines and embodies are Euro-American values. For example, it assumes that individuals, including children, are autonomous individuals; it makes little allowance for the different kinds of norms about children and raising children that exist across the globe; and it gives families and communities little say in the outcome of child placement. As we saw in Chapter 1, definitions and expectations of family, family formation, and parenthood differ across societies. Nevertheless, the Hague Convention uses self-described "universal" principles in its design of intercountry adoption. Thus, just as the West has had a larger role in the direction of how the world economy is globalized, it has had the largest voice in how intercountry adoptions should proceed. As one scholar argues, this Western voice has had important consequences:

> Western normative rationality with regard to the meaning of children, childhood, parenthood and families is exported [to] the many countries that send children to the west. . . . [The] motive is, in most cases, a genuine desire to improve conditions for children in the Third World in ways which go far beyond mere economic development and, hence, alert the citizens in these countries to (Western) rationality, morality, and the discourse of rights. . . . As such, the effort reveals clear overtone of the "white man's burden." Such a moral crusade absolves those involved from the need to seek enlightenment about indigenous . . . values; in their humanitarian quest, local practices are easily rendered irrelevant. (Howell 2006:12–13)

Thus, while the intentions of the Hague Convention are positive—to protect the children—the form it takes can be seen as reflecting distinctive Western values, to the exclusion of other values.

Some countries have tried to resist this dominant voice concerning intercountry adoption. For example, a group of African countries worked together to pass the African Charter on Rights and Welfare of the Child in 1986, arguing that children should not be considered merely individuals but, rather, part of communities. Those social relations, the African Charter asserted, should be taken into account in any adoption decision. In that way, this agreement resembles the Indian Child Welfare Act discussed in the last chapter. That act, too, insisted that children need to be seen as vital to entire communities and that their place in the wider community or group needs to be taken into account in any adoption. But even though there has been some resistance to the universalizing approach of the Hague

Convention, it has also become the dominant and most relied on model for transnational adoption.

In the next sections, after a brief overview of the history of transnational adoption, we focus on two receiving countries (Norway and the United States) and four sending countries (Korea, Guatemala, Romania, and China) to examine a range of issues relating to transnational adoptions. While each sending and receiving country is different in its participation in the processes of transnational adoptions, reflecting the particular social, political, and economic contexts in sending and receiving societies and in the interactions of both sides to the movement of children from one place to another, looking at these six countries nevertheless allows us to see some of the variations and similarities among countries across the globe. We take up the experience of adopted children and their families postadoption in a later section of this chapter.

The Receiving Countries

Early International Adoption as Humanitarian Aid

While adoption of children from other societies has undoubtedly taken place for a long time, the earliest modern transnational adoptions took place in response to country and world crises that left children homeless and orphaned. After the end of World War I, countries in Europe and North America sought to find a solution to the number of displaced people and did so through adjustment of or exceptions to existing immigration laws. In the United States, the adoption of children from other countries officially began in 1918 when Congress passed the Displaced Persons Act. While not all displaced persons were children or, especially, orphaned children, these children were part of the focus for many countries. Thus, as part of the settlement of displaced persons, 3,000 displaced orphans entered the United States; each had an American sponsor who did not necessarily adopt the child but did promise to care for the child properly. This act was temporary but, over the course of the following several decades, was renewed periodically. However, during the years preceding World War II, very few children were adopted from overseas; between 1935 and 1948, only 14 children entered the United States as adoptees (Adamec and Pierce 2000:165). While the humanitarian response was an important part of these adoptions, countries such as the United States were careful to construct laws and acts that did not threaten their existing immigration restrictions. Until the early 1960s, all adoptions of children from other countries by U.S. citizens occurred under refugee legislation and in response to specific crises (Lovelock 2000) and did not challenge immigration restrictions then in place in the United States.

World War II brought even greater attention to the need to help people displaced by war, although immigration restrictions continued to play a role. Canada permitted a relatively small number (about 2,000) of orphaned children to be adopted but restricted those adoptions to European children (Lovelock 2000). New Zealand also permitted adoptions of children displaced and orphaned by the war, but most of the children adopted (or fostered) to New Zealand were from Britain. In the United States, Congress permitted some international adoptions after the war ended. Children came to the United States mainly from Poland, Germany, Czechoslovakia, and Hungary, but some 2,400 children were adopted from Asia at that time, with two thirds of them coming from Japan (Schulman and Behrman 1993).

In the early years after World War II, the U.S. government permitted overseas adoptions only by military members. Thus, in 1953, Congress granted 500 special visas for orphans of any nationality to be adopted by American servicemen or government employees. Later that year, the Refugee Relief Act expanded that number, permitting 4,000 orphans to be adopted by these same groups, and in 1957, Congress removed the limit on the number of orphan visas granted. From that time on, the number of children adopted from outside the United States grew significantly. Between 1954 and 1958 some 10,000 children were adopted from other countries, especially from Germany, Japan, and Korea, by U.S. military personnel (Lovelock 2000). Canada, on the other hand, continued to restrict the entry and adoption of non-European children until 1962 (Lovelock 2000); New Zealand began to allow the adoption of children from Asia in 1963. Thus, among Western nations, the United States had some of the most inclusive rules about the nations from which children could be adopted but more restrictive rules about the pool of adopting parents. However, over the course of the 1950s, Congress gradually expanded the laws about who was permitted to adopt from outside the country. It was in 1961 that Congress passed the permanent Immigration and Nationality Act, opening up transnational adoption to any American who qualified.

Adoptions in the first half of the twentieth century were generally seen as humanitarian responses to crises; their purpose was to permit Americans and citizens of other wealthy nations to provide aid to countries through the act of adoption. But there were other, more implicit goals as well. Some Americans saw adoption of foreign children as a way to increase and improve relations with other countries, showing how Americans accepted the new responsibilities that came with their increased global power (Klein 2003). Some believed adoption could even be seen as a way to counter the threat of Communism; by adopting nonwhite children into their families, Americans showed their inclusiveness and humanitarian instincts, something that the world could see stood in stark contrast to Communist ideology, which, these Americans argued, promoted the destruction of family life (Klein 2003).

By the late 1950s, the motivation for international adoptions began to change in the United States and other Western nations. Certainly transnational adoption is often considered at least partly a humanitarian gesture. Thus, the sad and disturbing images of sick and lonely children in Romania's orphanages or the numbers of abandoned girls in China have helped to motivate adoptions from those countries, and many in the receiving countries speak in these instances and others of the importance of providing a loving home to a needy child. But increasingly, international adoption also has begun to be viewed as a solution to the increasing shortage of healthy white infants available for adoption domestically. Thus, the primary motivation and focus of these adoptions has shifted from the situation of children in need to the needs of adopting parents.

Figure 5.2 Transnational adoption works across a gradient of inequality. The United States, France, Spain, and Norway are among the receiving countries, with a large number and/or high rate of adoption of children from other countries. China, Guatemala, South Korea, the Russian Federation, and the Ukraine are among the sending countries, with the highest number of children adopted by foreigners.

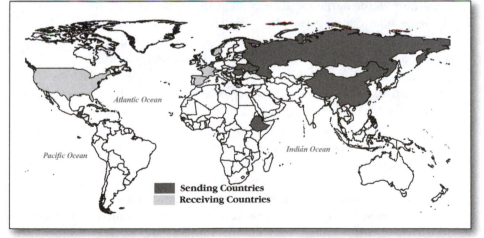

The United States

In the United States, transnational adoptions increased especially dramatically during the 1990s, rising from just over 7,000 in 1990 to over 20,000 by 2006 (see Figure 5.1). During these years, the number of countries from which children were adopted also grew, although China has dominated as a sending country in the past several years (see Table 5.1). While the United States signed the Hague Convention only in 2007, the U.S. government nevertheless has been actively engaged in trying to maintain tight control over who is allowed to adopt, from which localities, and under which rules.

What accounts for the changing interest in adoption of children from other countries? Here again, we can see that political, economic, and military events shaped both growing interest in and acceptance of these adoptions by those in receiving nations. Prior to the 1960s, as we have seen, American adoption practices followed a model in which parents and adopting children were matched by race, religion, and physical characteristics; such matching was seen as paramount to a successful family life, and adoption of children from other countries was seen as going against that model. The supply of children was also a key factor. Beginning in the late 1950s and early 1960s, there was a decreasing number of healthy American infants available for adoption. Wider distribution and more effective means of birth control, and later, changing laws that permitted abortion, meant that women had more control over their pregnancies and births. Fewer babies were born whose parents could not or did not want to raise them. Around the same time, the stigma attached to single motherhood lessened, allowing single mothers to keep children who might have been placed for adoption in earlier times.

A third factor in the increase in adoptions from outside the country is changing immigration laws. U.S. immigration laws restricted nearly all such adoptions as part of the wider immigration restrictions in place. Only with change in both the preferred adoption model and immigration law could international adoption take place. Local practices worked hand in hand with national policies; it was partly because of the pressure from child welfare and adoption groups that the U.S. government began to shift its immigration policies concerning adoption. (Similar pressures were behind shifts in overseas adoption policies in Canada and New Zealand.) At the same time, shifts at the global level were important; as we saw, the changing role of the United States in the global community after World War II forced a rethinking of American relations with and responsibilities to U.S. neighbors and allies. As the United States expanded its influence across the world, it developed new ties and allies, such as those with

Korea, and these relationships precipitated later adoption channels. We will return to many of these issues later in this chapter, when we look more closely at the adoption of Chinese girls by Americans.

Adoption in Norway

Norway shares many characteristics with the United States regarding adoption. It, too, is a rich country that has seen an increasing number of transnational adoptions; early adoptions, after World War II, were also humanitarian gestures to give needy and displaced children new homes. But there are also key differences between Norway and the United States, and looking at transnational adoption in Norway allows us insight into the norms of family building in that society. On a per capita basis Norway ranks as a country with one of the highest rates of transnational adoption in the world. In Norway, as in many other industrialized countries, international adoptions greatly outnumber domestic adoptions (e.g., in 2005, 75 percent of adoptions in Australia were transnational; Gibson 2006). This imbalance of domestic and international adoptions was not always the case: In 1965, international adoptions made up only a small percentage of all adoptions in Norway, and in 1980, only about a third of all adoptions were international. By 1991, those numbers had reversed, and two thirds of adoptions were international. By 2001, international adoptions constituted 75 percent of all adoptions (Norwegian Directorate for Children, Youth, and Family Affairs, www.bufetat.no). Even those numbers do not tell the whole story because nearly all domestic adoptions are adoptions of stepchildren by newly marrying parents. Transnational adoption is particularly important in countries such as Norway because there are virtually no Norwegian children available for adoption (i.e., by adults who are not related to them: so-called stranger adoptions). As we mentioned in an earlier chapter, Norway provides such a broad range and extensive set of social services (free birth control to all, abortion on demand, no stigma for single parents, and generous public financial support for children) that virtually all children born in Norway are raised by their birth parents. At the same time, infertility rates are fairly high in Norway, affecting 10 to 15 percent of all couples. (These infertility rates are likely caused by women's later age of marriage and childbearing and the declining quality of male sperm; Howell 2006.)

In Norway, where having a child is nearly imperative for all married couples, nearly all Norwegian couples who adopt do so because of involuntary childlessness (Howell 2006). Less a way to fulfill maternal instinct or a desire to reproduce oneself, adoption allows couples entry into the culture of the family. In contemporary Norwegian society, a normal family consists of children; without children, couples report, they remain outsiders to the main social networks of their communities (Howell 2001). While transnational adoption results in families that look unlike biological families, it opens up those necessary and important connections and allows parents access to what they perceive to be a normal life and a social community.

Adoption in Norway is closely monitored and shaped by state intervention, in both inclusive and exclusive ways. The adoption process is lengthy, usually requiring at least three years from start to finish. Norway, with its generous social services and general openness toward sexual practices, has some of the most restrictive policies in Europe when it comes to both new reproductive technologies and adoption. Thus, couples unable to bear children face additional hurdles. While sperm can be donated by a third party, neither egg donation nor surrogacy is permitted (Howell 2006:23). Thus, couples who want a child but are either unable or unwilling to bear a biological child must adopt, and because so few children are available for adoption domestically, couples adopt from other countries. The state is relatively restrictive in another aspect of family building: Adoption is generally permitted in Norway only for couples who are unable to bear a child biologically. Generally, it is only married women who are permitted to adopt, and in that way, those who fall outside a particular version of family are not allowed to create families through adoption. At the same time, government subsidies in Norway permit families from a wide range of incomes to adopt, and while adoption is expensive in Norway, it is about half as expensive as in the United States. A transnational adoption costs about the price of a new car in the United States but, because of government subsidy, about half the price of a new car in Norway. For all of these reasons, rates of adoption do not differ by socioeconomic status as they do in the United States; couples from all walks of life are just as likely to adopt in Norway.

The largest number of adoptees comes to Norway from China, followed by South Korea, Colombia, and Ethiopia (Howell and Marre 2006). Norwegian officials carefully oversee adoptions, and prospective adopting parents are not permitted to make certain kinds of requests relating to the characteristics of children. While they may request a particular country of origin and an age range and have some input about the extent of disability they are comfortable with, they are not allowed to express their preference for sex or skin color, as is possible in countries such as the United States (Howell 2006; Howell and Marre 2006). Adoption officials believe that families, even those formed through adoption, should have some element of chance and that such requests suggest gender or racial biases that cannot be permitted in this process.

The Sending Countries

The countries from which adopted children come share many common characteristics. Most of them are poor, and all of them are poor relative to the richer receiving countries (see Table 5.2). Many of the countries are in the midst of crises or strife, often caused by war. The combination of traumatic events and high levels of poverty result in situations wherein many children are orphaned and other children cannot be cared for properly by their families. In other circumstances, these children might have been adopted by neighbors or family members, but the dire circumstances—including poverty and displacement—that many find themselves in do not permit such outcomes. Adoption by foreigners who are wealthier, have more resources, and can provide a stable environment becomes one of the obvious and preferred options. But for international adoptions to take place, the sending country has to have in place some mechanism for identifying, verifying, and processing abandoned or orphaned children and a system through which prospective parents can be matched with those children. For many countries, putting such systems into place is more than they can handle in the midst of the other, more immediate needs of the country. One way these systems are set up is through the help of outsiders; foreign countries that are interested in assisting poorer countries are often able and willing to help find ways to cope with children who are abandoned, needy, or otherwise at risk. While adoption by foreigners might be one solution, more often, foreign aid helps with the creation of orphanages, with food distribution, and sometimes with the kind of infrastructure, economic support, and public health systems that allow birth parents to hold on to their children and raise them successfully, thus reducing the number of children who end up abandoned. In looking at the situations of four countries—Korea, Romania, Guatemala, and China—we see how transnational adoption has played a role in dealing with children who are in need.

Korea

Transnational adoptions began in Korea because of the Korean War of the early 1950s and its aftermath. The war left thousands of abandoned children, some who were orphaned by the war and others whose parents were unable to care for them. The earliest adoptees from Korea were often biracial, the children of foreigners (often servicemen) and Korean women. These children, whose parentage was often discernible in their looks, faced discrimination in a society made up almost entirely of one ethnicity. It was considered a humanitarian gesture to take those children from a potentially hostile environment and settle them in other countries. Later, other children who were not necessarily biracial but who were without parents were also among adopted Koreans. Once this route between Korea and other nations had begun, adoptions continued so that long after the Korean War ended, large numbers of Korean children were adopted by foreigners. Most Korean adoptees settled in the United States, but others went to Canada, Norway, Sweden, and other countries. What began as a humanitarian effort directed specifically to the damages caused by the war and its aftermath became something quite different the further from that war it got. Somewhere around 150,000 Korean children have been adopted by foreigners (nearly 100,000 by Americans) since these overseas adoptions began in 1953; over the past 50 years, Korean adoptees have constituted the largest proportion of internationally adopted children in the world (Johnson 2002). Within Korea, international adoptions have far outpaced domestic adoptions; during those same years, around 60,000 Korean children have been adopted within Korea (Lee 2007:79). The number of Koreans adopted by foreigners was influenced by several changes both within Korea and in receiving countries such as the United States. As we explained earlier, with fewer babies placed for adoption domestically, couples in industrialized countries wishing to adopt found it increasingly difficult to find adoptable babies in their own countries and began to look beyond their borders to build families. One of the reasons that Americans looking to adopt are attracted to Korean adoptees is that they believe children are well cared for before the adoption; many birth mothers live in maternity homes throughout pregnancy, and their children are placed in foster care (rather than in institutions, as in other countries such as China) after birth until they are adopted.

There were changes occurring in Korea too, affecting the number and origins of children needing adoption placement. After the initial war orphans, from the late 1950s through the 1970s, the children adopted from Korea were more often the children of single mothers or of poor urban families. While most of the children adopted (either domestically or internationally) in the 1970s were abandoned, only 8 percent of those adopted in 1998 were children who were abandoned (Lee 2007). Today, around 90 percent of children available for adoption in Korea are premarital births, many of them the babies of young women still in school (Lee 2007:5; see also Hübinette 2007). These changes suggest that the reasons for the relinquishment of children in Korea have shifted from poverty to unwanted pregnancies among unmarried women.

In recent years, the Korean government has tried to reduce the number of children adopted from Korea. In 1988, South Korea hosted the Olympics, and its out-adoptions received attention from the foreign press, which labeled Korea "the leading global exporter of children" (Hübinette 2007:118). That attention embarrassed the country and the government and led to more restrictions placed on foreign adoptions of Korean children and an effort to increase domestic adoptions.

Nevertheless, Korea continues to send around 2,000 children a year to foreign countries for adoption. While it was the United States's involvement in Korea during and after the war that led Americans to consider adopting Korean children, it is family expectations and norms within Korea that lead to the continuing practice of abandoning Korean children who subsequently need homes. Koreans have been reluctant to adopt unrelated children because of the strong influence of Confucianism on family structure; in that system, blood ties and family lineage are important aspects of family continuity and success. Nevertheless, there have been changes within Korea that have led to fewer children being placed for adoption and to a larger percentage of children adopted domestically rather than internationally (Lee 2007). In 2002, of the more than 4,000 adoptions that were enacted in Korea, around 41 percent (1,694) took place domestically (Lee 2007:79). While the government is working to reduce the number of children adopted by foreigners, there are still barriers to domestic adoption. There is still reluctance to adopting a child outside of one's bloodline, and these kinds of barriers, coupled with the long history of international adoption, suggest that transnational adoptions from Korea are likely to continue in the near future.

Romania

For much of the 1990s, Romania was the source of many international adoptions. In these transnational exchanges of children, we see how the domestic policies of a sending country interact with the desires of prospective parents in other countries and result in a large number of adoptions, many of which are considered problematic in several ways.

From 1965 to 1989, Romania was ruled by Nicolae Ceaucescu. Dismayed by Romania's declining fertility rate, he believed that for the country to be strong and able to garner respect on the world stage, it would have to increase its population. To bolster population growth, women were encouraged to have many children, sex education was banned, and several laws were passed that restricted access to the means of family planning; abortion was completely outlawed, and birth control access was highly restricted. The consequences for women were harsh, particularly for those with no access to black-marketed services; unable to control when and how many children to bear, women endured unwanted pregnancies and births (Dickens 2002). Many of the children ended up in state institutions as parents were unable or unwilling to care for them. Lacking resources and funding, these institutions were often in terrible condition, and the children who were housed there were neglected and in poor health. Even after the fall of Ceaucescu in 1989, the situation in Romania remained grim; widespread poverty meant that parents continued to be unable to care adequately for their children.

With the collapse of Ceaucescu's government in 1989, the foreign press had increased access to Romania. It began to publish reports of these institutions and unwanted children. Westerners responded immediately and with great passion to these stories. In some cases, people wanted to travel to Romania to rescue a child or children from these institutions. Others saw in this situation a new source of potentially adoptable children, children who were usually white and fair skinned. Westerners rushed to Romania and began long and sometimes difficult adoption proceedings. On its part, the Romanian government saw international adoption as a way to rid itself of unwanted (and sometimes disabled or ill) children. But there was little structure within the country to handle adoption, creating a situation ripe for corruption and illegal practices. In addition, it was often difficult to tell if a child in an institution was there permanently or had been placed there only temporarily as the parents sought a way to support him or her.

The combination of unwanted births, poverty, desperate foreigners looking to adopt, and a corrupt political system led to an adoption crisis in Romania. While there were some legitimate agencies involved in placing children for adoption, there were also many private agencies and individuals who became involved in baby selling and buying, encouraging Romanian mothers to sell their babies for international adoption. During the 1990s, foreigners adopted approximately 30,000 Romanian babies (Laffan 2005). Foreigners became complicit—knowingly and unknowingly—in corrupt and unethical adoption practices. Because going through state channels could result in slow and unsuccessful adoptions, many foreigners turned to private sources within Romania that were "more expensive, very arbitrary, and subject to unsavory practices of coercion, corruption, and foreign complicity" (Kligman 1992:411). While foreign adoptive parents sometimes fell victim in this chaos, even more vulnerable were poor Romanian women (especially Roma or Gypsy women) who were often coerced into relinquishing their children for international adoption. In some of these cases, mothers were offered sums of money to relinquish their children, and hard-pressed poor women sometimes felt they had little alternative but to sign away their children (Kligman 1992). In cases in which adoptive parents were caught between the looser Romanian and more rigorous U.S. laws concerning adoptable children, they sometimes appealed to their congressperson to help them get approval to adopt. It is not always clear how much knowledge the foreign adoptive parents had of the behind-the-scenes practices, but as one critic of these processes made clear, some may have been aware:

> Even though adoptive parents may have intuited something was amiss, they nonetheless chose not to know. In view of the language barrier, lack of knowledge was easy to rationalize although it cannot absolve them of responsibility. To have allowed themselves to know meant that they would have had to succumb to their own emotional pain at the loss of a child with whom they may have already bonded. It was easier to believe, whatever the temporary circumstances, that adoption was simply for the good of the child who would escape the hardships of life in Romania. (Kligman 1992:414)

The difference in resources—economic and political—between adopting and birth parents is stark here and underscores how looking at transnational adoptions through the eyes of birth parents or adoptive parents gives very different perspectives on these processes.

Bowing to international pressure that focused on the ethical issues involved in these practices, Romania's new government changed its adoption practices in 1991. All private adoptions were banned; adoptions were permitted only from government institutions and only if the children were truly orphaned or abandoned. In 2001, Romania stopped all foreign adoptions and began to revamp how it handled abandoned children. As of early 2011, Romania continues its ban on foreign adoption; only two children were adopted from Romania by Americans in 2008 (romania.adoption.com). Nevertheless, the controversy over unwanted children continues in Romania; even though birth control and abortion are more widely available, parents continue to abandon children in large numbers and the state struggles to care for them. UNICEF reported that in 2005, 9,000 babies were abandoned at either maternity wards or pediatric hospitals (Ionescu 2005). The government is attempting to find ways to force families to take back these abandoned children, but like the state, the parents often do not have the resources to care for them. Thus, a paradox of international adoption is clearer: While it is fraught and entwined with serious problems, it is a way for a poor country to deal with a large number of abandoned children for whom there are few resources at home.

Guatemala

In many ways, in terms of adoption, Guatemala shares characteristics with Romania. Guatemala is a relatively poor country, and it has a history of foreign adoption. Unlike Romania, the government has never tried to increase fertility or population size; rather, it sees its population as growing too rapidly. Nevertheless, the combination of poverty and a demand for children from outside its borders has led to charges of baby trafficking in Guatemala as well.

Over the past decade, the number of transnational adoptions from Guatemala has been rising, especially adoptions to the United States. In 1997, 788 Guatemalan children were adopted by Americans; this figure rose to 2,219 by 2002 and to 4,000 by 2006, making Guatemalan children the third largest group of foreign adoptees arriving in the United States that year, after Chinese and Russian children (http://www.travel.state.gov/family/adoption/stats). On the Guatemalan side, it is estimated that 98 percent of all adoptions are to foreigners (and 62 percent of those are to Americans; Wilson and Gibbons 2005:743). Guatemala has the highest per capita rate of out-adoption of any country in the world. Americans are drawn to adopting children from Guatemala because of the lower costs, the country's proximity to the United States, and the relatively shorter duration of as well as lack of red tape in the adoption process.

In late 2007, the Guatemalan government temporarily suspended all adoptions by foreigners as it attempted to get control of a process that appeared to be turning into a baby-buying and -selling market; as of early 2011, international adoptions were still on hold. Potential adopting parents in the United States are disturbed by the shutdown, particularly those who were in the middle of the adoption process when the Guatemalan government stepped in. One mother who had adopted a baby from Guatemala in the past and was planning to adopt a second, withdrew from the process for fear that it would be stopped midway. But she remains bothered when she sees photos of Guatemalan children without homes. "You look at each one and think: 'If we don't commit to him, what's going to happen to him? Is he ever going to get a family? Is he going to end up begging on the street?' . . . It's heart-wrenching" (Aizenman and Roig-Franzia 2007:B01).

But those in Guatemala see it differently. One official lamented, "Guatemala has converted into a baby-producing nation. . . . Our children come into this world to be products for sale. . . . It's as if they were a car. What model is it? And who wants to buy it?" (Aizenman and Roig-Franzia 2007:B01). As in Romania, it is a mix of poverty in the sending country, the desire of parents-to-be in the receiving countries, and a lack of government regulation that come together to encourage unethical practices. Poverty is rampant in Guatemala, especially among the indigenous populations. As in Romania, private agencies and individuals have filled the gap created by the lack of government regulatory agencies. These agencies can make an adoption relatively easy for a foreign couple, who is often able to adopt a very young baby; some of the babies have been identified by intermediaries as adoptable even before birth. And as in Romania, there are charges that women, particularly poor women, are being coerced through offers of money to relinquish their children for foreign adoption. There are also charges that some women are bearing children with the intention of selling them in the adoption market.

China and Its Abandoned Girls

Adoptions from China, like those from Romania, are partly the result of both the kind of state involvement in reproductive politics in the country that has influenced parents' ability or willingness to raise the children they bear and a decision to allow foreigners to adopt abandoned children.

China sends more children out of the country for adoption than any other country; a large percentage of those children end up in the United States (Selman 2006). Of all the children adopted internationally in the United States in 2007, 28 percent were born in China (U.S. State Department, www.adoption.state.gov). This practice got under way in the 1990s, after China passed a law outlining the process for the adoption of children by foreigners; prior to that date, there were relatively few children adopted from China by foreigners. But the number of adoptions of Chinese children by Americans has increased rapidly; between 1991 and 2007, over 48,500 Chinese children were adopted from China (U.S. Embassy-China, http://guangzhou.usembassy-china.org.cn/adoption.html).

While exact numbers are not known, by all reports, there are vast numbers of abandoned children in China, most of them housed in state institutions. Most of the healthy babies who have been abandoned are girls, and therein lies a major clue as to what is happening in China today. In 1980, the Chinese state enacted a restrictive and sweeping birth-planning policy. This policy restricts the number and timing of all births in China; in urban areas, couples are allowed only one child, while in rural areas, couples are usually permitted two children. This policy came on top of a strong preference for sons and created a situation of abandoned and missing girls. Parents feel they need a son—to carry on the family line and to provide for support in old age. Families are patrilineal in China, and thus only males are counted as true descendants of any family. Families are also patrilocal, meaning that girls leave their families and often their villages and move into their husbands' families and villages at marriage, making daughters unavailable for old age care. With restrictions on how many children they can have, couples sometimes choose to abandon a baby daughter to try again to have the necessary son. The result has been thousands and thousands of "missing girls"—girls who have been abandoned, whose births have not been reported, who have been killed at birth, or who were never born because of sex-selective abortions.

Transnational adoptions draw from the pool of children who end up in state institutions. While the number of these adoptions by foreigners has been growing steadily since the mid-1990s, they constitute only a small percentage of all institutionalized children. As we discussed in Chapter 3, Chinese couples, both in the past and currently, have been ready to adopt, some even preferring to adopt girls. But most of these adoptions are informal, not passing through the state. Reluctant to allow Chinese couples to adopt abandoned girls, the Chinese state turned to international adoption to help clear its overcrowded orphanages (Johnson 2002). While there were some domestic adoptions from these state institutions, they were relatively few, particularly so as the number of international adoptions grew during the 1990s. In fact, around the same time that the state made it possible for foreigners to adopt Chinese children, it placed severe restrictions on the adoption of children by domestic couples, limiting adoption to only those over 35 who were unable to give birth. The question here is why the state chose the route of international rather than domestic adoption. While it is true that international adoption did bring some revenue into China, particularly to welfare institutions that took care of abandoned children, the amount of income this process generated was relatively insignificant. A more likely explanation is that the Chinese state was concerned that allowing Chinese couples to adopt these abandoned children might represent a loophole in the state's plan to restrict births and lower fertility and population growth. Some government officials worried that couples might abandon a girl to have a biological boy, with the intention of adopting a girl at a later date.

Americans adopt Chinese children (nearly all of them girls) in great numbers. In 2009, 3,001 (down from a high of 7,902 in 2005) children were adopted from China by Americans (http://www.travel.state.gov/family/adoption/stats). Chinese children are also adopted by parents in other countries such as Norway and Sweden. One of the major reasons that American parents have looked to China for adoption is the simple availability of children. The process, while lengthy and expensive, has also not been subject to the same criticisms or concerns about unethical practices or corruption as have adoption processes in places such as Romania or Guatemala. (Although there have been occasional concerns about these issues in past years, they have never reached the level seen in other countries.) In addition, until recently, China permitted adoptions by foreigners who were often rejected by other countries because of age or marital status. For that reason, older couples and single parents turned to China for children. For many years, Chinese officials seemed to turn a blind eye to the sexual orientation of potential adopting parents as well; for that reason, many lesbians and lesbian couples looked to China to adopt a child. In 2007, China passed more restrictive regulations about who is allowed to adopt Chinese children. Potential adopting parents must be married (for at least two years), be in good health, and not be overweight. These restrictions are bound to influence which prospective American parents end up adopting children from China.

The place and meaning of Chinese adoption in American society is complicated. One author has called American adoptions of Chinese babies since the 1990s "one of the most visible expression of . . . American willingness to hybridize. . . . These adoptions showed America's increasing ties to Asia and have become one of the ways in which Americans live globalization in their everyday lives" (Klein 2003:270–71). Indeed, these adoptions happen in a very different way and in a different world than did early Korean adoptions. While many Americans rue the plight of Chinese baby girls, these adoptions are not usually seen as purely humanitarian gestures. Part of the explanation is that China is not seen as a country needing to be saved by Americans. By the 1990s, when Chinese international adoptions began, China, while poor, was an increasingly powerful nation and one that the United States could not easily dominate. Thus, Americans have a different relationship with Asia today than they did 50 years ago. Nevertheless, in discussions of Chinese adoptions or of China more generally, we see continuing elements of orientalism, of fear of China as an unknown and dangerous power, exotic and mysterious. Americans continue to have a love/hate relationship with China, seeing China as both friend and potential enemy, and this contradictory stance has influenced the adoptions of Chinese children as well. Looking at adoptions of Chinese by Americans, as we do below, allows us to see how American attitudes have changed since the 1950s and 1960s and how they continue to reflect earlier understandings of Asia.

Our examination of the processes of transnational adoption has allowed us to see how specific social, political, economic, and historical experiences play a role in both sending and receiving societies around adoption. Whether it is the role of restrictive birth-planning policies in Romania or China, the widespread poverty in Guatemala, or state control over adoption in Norway, elements in each situation shape adoption processes. Indeed, receiving countries nearly always have particular relationships—historical, political, or economic—that facilitate the sending and receiving of children across borders; these relationships are nearly always unequal. Very few children move from the global South to the global North, and parents in rich countries do not often adopt children in other rich countries.

These relationships are part of all adoption processes, at both the societal and individual level. While adoption is obviously a very individual, intimate, and private process, the transitions and experiences of adopted children and their families are deeply connected to the larger global processes and relationships as well. As one scholar describes this process, "transnational adoption pulls into proximity broad political economic forces with the intimate realms of kinship" (Kim 2007:590). We next turn to look at what happens after transnationally adopted children arrive in their new homes and countries.

After Adoption:
The Making of Transnational Families

Whether or not the implicit race and ethnicity issues involved in this kind of family making are an explicit part of the adoption process, most of those involved in transnational adoptions will eventually have to face them. While some adoptees (e.g., those from eastern Europe) might be white, many are of a different race or ethnicity than their usually white parents. Whether or not these family members themselves consider this racial/ethnic difference to be important, in daily life the adoptee and his or her family members are likely to confront racial stereotypes and doubts from outsiders about whether theirs is a "real" family. In this way, they may share experiences of transracial families, where children of races different from the parents' races are adopted from within the United States. But in addition to these issues, transnationally adopted children deal with the meaning of having a different country of birth than their family members. As one scholar of such adoptions notes, these adoptees are always connected to two places, sometimes in complicated and even contradictory ways (Yngvesson 2005). In this section, we particularly highlight the experience of Chinese children adopted by American parents; in recent years, this group of transnational adoptees has received more attention than most other groups. This attention is due in part to the sheer size of this group: a large number of transnational adoptees, of the same gender and approximately the same age, within a relatively short time. While some of their experiences are unique to their background and arrival into the country, many of their experiences, and the larger issues that have surfaced around their adoptions, are shared by most transnational adoptees and their families.

Transnational adoptions are handled very differently by most families today than they were in the 1950s, 1960s, and even 1970s. The American parents of children adopted from Korea during those decades were often instructed by adoption officials not to discuss or dwell on the children's origins. Raised not only in white homes but often in predominantly white communities, these children were not given the freedom or encouragement (or, some might say, burden) to explore their birth cultures or their relationships to them. The goal at that time was racial assimilation. It is not surprising, therefore, that in a survey of Korean adoptees (reported in Freundlich and Lieberthal 2000), over a third of females and nearly half of males adopted from Korea stated that they thought of themselves as white. This survey found that many adoptees struggled with being Korean or Asian versus being white, describing themselves as they were growing up as "Amerasian trying to be 'white,'" "not 'white' enough," and "Caucasian, except when looking in the mirror [when] I was reminded that I was Korean." Others stated that as they were growing up, they saw themselves as Caucasian or white. These adoptees described themselves as "Caucasian who happened to look different," "Caucasian with a difference," "a white person in an Asian body," and "white middle class, but adopted from Korea" (Freundlich and Lieberthal 2000:7–8).

Today, adopting families are usually counseled by adoption officials on the issues of race, nationality, and the ambiguity of belonging simultaneously to two places at once; they are encouraged to learn about the child's culture and to maintain some connection to that culture. Much of that change comes from the shifting social landscape as Americans have more contact with cultures different from their own and as identity politics and the celebration of difference have taken hold in many communities. While controversy continues over whether immigrants should strive for cultural assimilation, the maintenance of cultural ties, or some combination, there is at any rate a public conversation about these issues. Many parents of Chinese adoptees are older, are well educated, and because of their single status or sexual orientation (until recently China allowed single, lesbian, and gay parents to adopt) are often themselves seen as outside the normal family mold. They thus bring to the adoption complex understandings and experiences about difference and belonging.

Watching the 1999 World Cup women's soccer finals, the McCarthy family— white parents and their adopted Chinese daughter Peggy—were riveted as they watched China and the United States fight to the end to determine who would win the World Cup. With a tie score, it looked like the final score would be decided by a penalty kick. As the American Brandi Chastain kicked the penalty shot and cleared the goal, the crowd went wild. So too did the McCarthys, watching the game at home on the television. But not

five seconds after the three cheered the American victory, Peggy—pulled
between her identities as Chinese and American—began to cry out of disap-
pointment that although "her" team, USA, had won, "her" team, China,
had lost. (From authors' personal notes)

Peggy's contradictory feelings about something as relatively unimportant as
a soccer match are mirrored in the dual loyalties and identities of many
transnationally adopted children in ways that are present in various facets of
their lives.

Most children adopted from other societies are very aware of their dual
identities. In addition, media attention to these transnational adoptions—in
publications that range from *Newsweek* to *Ladies Home Journal* to *Parents
Magazine*—reflects the ways that today's society is more aware of and more
interested in discussing the issues concerning these adoptions. Adopting
parents themselves have formed groups, from groups addressing the logistics
and politics of adoption to playgroups and language groups and more. The
Internet has played an important role, allowing the sharing of information
and the formation of virtual communities of those who have gone through
similar experiences. For example, International Korean Adoption Service, or
InKAS, is an organization that provides a variety of services to Korean adoptees, most of them available online. Adoptees can sign up to travel to Korea
with other adoptees, can use the site's resources to begin searching for their
birth families, or can join a discussion group of Korean adoptees. Catering
to a different audience, Families with Children from China (FCC) has an
extensive website for adopting families. On its website, FCC describes itself
as "a nondenominational organization of families who have adopted children from China. The purpose of FCC is [to] provide a network of support
for families who've adopted in China and to provide information to prospective parents" (www.fwcc.org). The large number of first Korean and
later Chinese adoptees—and in the case of Chinese adoptees, their gender
and age similarities—has allowed the growth of organizations for both parents and adoptees and intensified media and scholarly attention.

But this changed environment does not mean that the issues of adoption
have been solved or that adoption, particularly transnational or transracial
adoption, has been openly embraced by the larger society. While awareness
and knowledge of birth cultures and connections between adoptees and their
birth cultures are obviously valuable, they also raise difficult and nearly
unsolvable questions and force us to confront complex issues.

Transnational, like transracial, families obviously and publicly challenge
the place of biology in forming kin bonds. Whereas in the past adoptive

children and parents were matched so that the adoptive family looked like a "normal" family, children adopted across racial, ethnic, and national lines force us to consider the ways that family bonds are constructed and how families can be formed in a variety of ways. In a children's book published in 1960 but still widely read, *Are You My Mother?* by P. D. Eastman, a little bird searches for his mother. In his search, it becomes clear that the characters in the book, and presumably the readers, assume that mothers and children look alike. A dog cannot be his mother because they look different, and neither can a hen or a car. He finds his mother and sees how they resemble each other. The message of this children's book contradicts the reality of families in which individual members look very different from one another. But while more and more families deviate from the norms of the past in the way they are constructed or appear, these changes are not completely accepted. Adoptive families face regular challenges to the authenticity of their families, with questions from strangers and friends alike: "Who is her real mother?" "How much did she cost?" and "What does her father look like?" Questions like these force these families to deal regularly with their difference, their difference from each other and from a still-expected family model.

It is partly in response to this forced recognition of difference that families have tried to provide their children an understanding of their origins and a sense of pride in their ethnicity and race. As well, many have learned from the questions and difficulties that Korean adoptees have publicly voiced about the impossibility of racial assimilation and the sadness they have expressed over their lack of Korean identity. For example, Beth Kyong Lo is a Korean American adopted by white parents who is now working as a psychologist with other Korean adoptees. She argues that Korean adoption in the 1960s and 1970s was generally seen as successful, with adoptees adjusting well to their new families and communities. However, Lo argues that adoptees' adjustment was often a careful response to the racism around them, "necessary for our survival in an environment we hoped would not re-abandon us" (2006:171). Because at that time part of successful adjustment to American communities was a denial of connections to Korean culture, it was only when they reached adulthood, she argues, that these adoptees felt free to explore their Korean identities and address their complex ethnic, national, and family pasts.

Developing a sense of belonging to one's birth culture is not a simple or straightforward task. If race and ethnicity are socially constructed, then in what ways are, or should, adopted children be tied to their birth cultures? They often leave those cultures in infancy, without language or memories from that first place. And the nods that adoptive parents make to that culture have been described by one scholar as "culture bites" (Anagnost 2000:413); they often involve celebrating national holidays, wearing national dress, or eating food from the country of birth (see Jacobsen 2008). Parents often buy trinkets, art, or other things from their children's birth cultures, outfitting their home or a room in these cultural objects (see Traver 2007; Kasimitz 2007 for discussions of the meaning of consumer purchases to adopting parents). While these may be markers of culture, removed as they are from the wider social and cultural context, they may have little meaning. Adopting parents rarely know very much about their children's culture and often begin to learn only once the adoption process is under way. Some critics of these attempts at cultural connections argue that they exoticize Chinese culture and ignore the complexities and controversies that make China a real, rather than a reified or "Disneyfied," place (Anagnost 2000; Volkman 2005). As one adopting mother wrote about what she imagined her life would be with her new Chinese daughter, "I had vague pictures of picking tea leaves on a mountainside while she babbled cheerfully in a sling. Contented, fulfilled, I would push her in a stroller along West Lake, soothed by the gentle lapping of water and the misty mountains in the distance" (McCabe 2003:3). While her trip to China to adopt her daughter forced her to replace those exoticized images of China with the realities of both motherhood and China itself, most people do not have the same kind of contact or opportunities that permit such a de-exoticizing.

At the same time, neither are these children the same as their white family members; outsiders see them as nonwhite and often expect them to have some knowledge of and connection to the other culture. Adopted Asians are thus confronted with the same issues and challenges that most Asians in the United States face. Asians in the United States—whether adopted or not, whether they have just arrived in the country or are fourth-generation immigrants—are expected to have connections to their motherland in a way that is different from the expectations for others, such as Italian Americans or even African Americans. How often are Italian Americans asked if they speak Italian? In some ways, the dilemmas around culture faced by transnational adoptees are similar to those of second- or third-generation immigrants; often they too have no memories of, and often have never been to, the motherland. But more often than Chinese or other transnational adoptees, they have grown up in families and communities with cultural, political, and economic ties to those places. Asian adoptees are subject to some of the same stereotyping and reactions as are other Asian Americans, seen as perpetual foreigners. That makes developing an identity tricky because Asians in the United States are constantly confronting the ways that others perceive them. One Asian American scholar describes the role of others in shaping his identity: "In most instances, I am who others perceive me to be rather than how I perceive myself to be" (Wu 2003:8).

Thus, adoptive families are caught in a dilemma. They must prepare their children for life in a racialized culture where nonwhites are subject to racial/ethnic stereotypes and discrimination. At the same time, as their children are growing up in a white family, many parents attempt to frame ethnic or racial difference in a positive way. "Nurturing 'cultural pride' is often seen as the critical ground on which later struggles against racism may be waged. The startling, sometimes shocking, discovery of racism, whether subtle or flagrant, has transformed many parents' consciousness of race in ways they never anticipated" (Volkman 2005:92). White parents of adopted nonwhite children are often forced to understand the importance of race and white privilege in ways new to them.

Some have argued that adopting families ignore Chinese American culture and the place of Chinese Americans in American society. One Chinese American woman warned,

> I fear that some parents might mistake the colorful trappings of Chinese traditions for the experience of being Chinese-American. . . . I can understand why parents are so intrigued by sword dancing, lantern making, dragon boat racing, and mooncake baking. These snippets of Chinese culture are appealing, fun, and just more accessible than grappling with the more difficult issue of identity and the race thing. (Quoted in Volkman 2005:93–94)

Chinese Americans and other Asian Americans have had to understand the complexities of a racialized United States, where they are often seen as a combination of yellow peril, model minority, and perpetual foreigner (Lee 1999). Eventually, as these Chinese adoptees move into young adulthood and later adulthood, they too will have to deal with these issues, if only because others usually see them not as Chinese adoptees but as Chinese Americans.

Nevertheless, for children adopted from China and elsewhere, their adopted status is also an important part of their identity. It may be that parents' search for connections to China (or Guatemala or Korea) are partly about a search for their family (rather than national) origins. Because China does not allow parents to relinquish children for adoption, babies are usually abandoned in an anonymous fashion. Thus, it is not likely that many Chinese adoptees will ever be able to find their birth parents, and a connection to the country or culture may act as a substitute for those birth ties, both for the child and for her adopting parents. While a child's personal history is not likely to ever be known, understanding the country's history might help to give the child a sense of her place in the world. Many argue that this may be as important for adopting parents as for their children as they struggle to find the proper place for their own mixed feelings about their children's origins. As one adoptive mother expressed, "I don't know what to say to a woman whose greatest tragedy is my good fortune" (Prager, quoted in Volkman 2005:86). Connections to the birth culture and even trips back to the country of birth help not only adopted children but their adopting parents make sense of the contradictory process of which they are a part.

Conclusions

Even as many of the struggles, joys, and challenges of these adoptions are experienced in intimate, private family spheres, transnational adoption and those involved in it bring to the public stage issues that many societies struggle with today: What constitutes a family? How important are blood ties? How important is looking alike to family cohesion and function? The ties to a birth culture that are now accepted and even encouraged in the United States suggest that adopted children do not arrive as blank slates. The movement of children in this globalized world comes out of a history of poverty, colonialism, economic ties, and political relationships between nations; this history leaves traces on the children who circulate and all others involved in the adoption. Children leave their places of origin under particular circumstances and arrive in their new homes to deal with the racialized, classed, and ideological issues of the time. They and their families must create kinship amid these histories and circumstances. Transnational adoption makes clear the ways that kinship is forged, not born.

Conclusion

On a recent flight to Beijing, one of the authors sat next to a woman, Clarice, who was on her way to China to adopt a baby girl. Clarice described the difficulties she had gone through in the process of arranging this transnational adoption. It had taken Clarice four years of work and waiting to get to this moment, the moment where she was now able to travel to China, go to the orphanage, and bring home her newly adopted daughter. Clarice spoke of the mixed feelings she had. On the one hand, she was tremendously excited; she described how she and the rest of her family (her husband and three biological children, who were traveling with her on this journey to China) felt elated. They talked about how they were doing the right thing. Clarice was sure that her family and this child would be better off; they were ready to give this child the family that any child deserved, and they themselves would benefit as much as the child would. But she also wondered about what she was doing, about how, while she believed she was doing the right thing, she also wasn't completely sure. She wondered, What does it mean to take a child from her culture and plant her in a very different one? What would it mean for a Chinese child to grow up in an all-white family? How was it that she benefitted from this process only because a mother in China was losing her child? Clarice and her family had spent many resources—time, money, energy—to get to this point. She worried that perhaps her daughter would grow up and resent having been pulled from her culture in this way. And she talked about how she hoped her daughter would understand that if it were not the right thing to do, Clarice had done it carefully and thoughtfully, and with the best intentions.

That conversation, taking place over the Pacific on the long flight to China from the United States, was a reminder of how adoption is always about individuals. Most adoptions happen only after enormous effort on the part of many people. And talking with this very thoughtful, compassionate woman was a reminder that in many cases this work includes soul searching, reflection, and questioning as birth and adopting parents, relatives and friends, adoption officials and courts try to decide what is the right thing to do—for the birth parents, for the adopting family, and for the child. What does it mean to keep the best interests of the child at the forefront of adoption decisions? It is often difficult to know, and the answers are rarely simple or easy to find.

Even as we keep in mind the individual people whose work and care are necessary for any adoption to take place, we also acknowledge that adoption is about much more than individuals. Employing a sociological imagination in examining the processes and practices of adoption allows us to recognize that adoptions are simultaneously about individuals, communities, societies, and the global world. Moreover, such a perspective enables us to shift between these points of focus without losing the sense that each is significant. Focusing on individuals, we can see how adoption fulfills significant needs and desires. In many societies, including the United States, raising children is a valued part of being an adult. Some adults may be unable or unwilling to bear a biological child and turn to adoption to find a child and to build a family. In other situations, adults other than parents may have rights to and obligations for raising children, temporarily or permanently, and most adults may view fosterage or adoption as the best and most successful way of raising children. For individuals who, for an array of social, political-economic, or personal circumstances, are unable or unwilling to care for and raise their own children, adoption and fosterage may allow a long-term solution that takes into account the well-being of the child as well. Finally, children who have lost their parents through death, abandonment, or other circumstances or have been removed from the care of their parents may find a new family, a mutually caring group of people with whom to live, through adoption or fosterage.

For the communities in which these individuals live and interact, adoption serves important functions as well. Raising children requires considerable resources on the part of individuals, the community, and the society: Time, money, knowledge, attention, commitment, and emotional engagement are all necessary pieces of raising children. If parents are unable to provide these resources, someone else must; in many places, this means that local, state, and/or federal governments or private entities support children. Adoption and fostering can relieve these systems of some of the pressures and may provide children with a richer environment and more stable community in which to make the transition to adulthood. As Native American proponents of the Indian Child Welfare Act have shown, communities also benefit from children through their very presence, through the role children play in maintaining and transforming cultural and communal life. Children and adults benefit from the interaction between generations and in contexts in which they feel safe and comfortable.

Adoption also speaks to larger social institutions and structures. Without a sociological lens, one that allows us to bring individual and societal perspectives into the picture, we would be unable to explain why some children, and not others, circulate among families; why some people adopt or foster children and others do not; and why some avenues for adoption or fosterage are available and other are not. We need that sociological imagination, then, to make sense of the patterns of adoption, both within particular societies and between them.

Throughout this book we have used a comparative perspective, which illuminates the role of adoption and other kinds of child circulation in countries outside the United States and underscores how adoption and child placement are interwoven with the social and cultural context. That context includes the role of children in the family and society, norms about family and family making, and the relationship between the community and family. Thus, in many west African societies children have long been raised by adults other than their biological parents. But not just any adult takes on the role of foster mother or foster father; usually the circulation of children helps to cement the relationships among family members who belong to the same patrilineal kinship group even though they may live far from each other in rural communities or urban neighborhoods. To be raised by people other than birth parents is both commonsense—for otherwise children would not develop the skills, strength, and emotional maturity they need as adults— and valuable to the maintenance of broader family ties. In other social and cultural contexts, different assumptions, ideals, and institutions correlate with different arrays of practice. As we saw, Muslim families are reluctant to adopt nonrelated children because of the ways that Islamic rules about families are interpreted, and Andean families are willing to foster the children of strangers because those children may eventually become kin through everyday practices such as the sharing of food and space.

The patterning of adoption and fostering is also evident at different historical periods in the United States. For instance, during the 1950s and 1960s, a nascent public system and private institutions supporting adoption enabled young white women who found themselves pregnant outside of marriage to deliver their children; these institutions encouraged them to relinquish their children for adoption and attempt to take up their old lives again. White married couples, who were looking for a way to have children without going through the biological process of birth, could also use this system to find children. For young black women, and women of other racial and ethnic minorities, these avenues were not available. With few adoption services available to blacks, and with a nonporous black/white color line, young women who were dealing with unplanned pregnancies and couples looking to adopt had to find other routes. Many African American families and communities responded by making provisions to help in these situations. Some unmarried mothers raised their children in their own family homes; some adults took on the task of raising children—their own and those of others—under difficult circumstances, but they nonetheless provided the resources, especially the time, love, and commitment, that the children needed to become adults. Whereas U.S. society stigmatized all girls who were pregnant but not married, white middle-class girls were urged to delay parenting, and black and poor girls were not. Recognizing the ways social and political-economic resources and relationships are structured within a society at large helps us to gain insight into the differing ideals of, and constraints on, individuals, families, and communities as they act to care for children.

When we look for patterns of adoption, we can see clearly how adoption follows lines of inequality within and across societies. From a certain angle, it makes sense that children would move from those families with fewer resources for rearing children to those with more resources. From another angle, the movement of children also illuminates the power relationships that structure societies and international relationships. When adoptive parents from a wealthier country, such as the United States or Norway, stress that a child from a poorer country, such as Guatemala, is better off with them, they ignore the lack of state support available to poor women for keeping and raising their own children should they so desire. Global political and economic relationships shape adoption and fostering practices, whether it is the educational and economic pressures that make it more likely that rural families in Benin send children to urban relatives or poverty and state violence that affect how well families can support children in the Andes.

Along with illuminating how certain children come to be adopted by particular adults within one society, bringing a sociological perspective to adoption helps us comprehend the complexities of global relationships, the intertwined dependencies and the cracks of inequality along which we all live in today's world. To highlight these mutually reinforcing hierarchies, Ana Teresa Ortiz and Laura Briggs (2003) suggest that we consider the various forms of adoption in the United States and how those connect to global relations of power. As we have discussed throughout the book, private adoptions, public or private agency adoptions, and transnational adoptions are all legitimate forms of adopting children, but they are also used by different adopting parents for different reasons. Looking at these different ways to build families through adoption also gives us clues about wider societal values and norms. In particular, Ortiz and Briggs compare transnational adoption from Romania and adoption from the American foster care system. In both cases, they argue, the children tend to be older and thus have some possibility of previous difficulties in their lives that might suggest future problems of adjustment. Adoption from Romania is more expensive and more difficult than domestic American adoption, and studies indicate that the extent of the problems that children have after adoption is similar for both groups of children. Why then, these authors ask, would parents choose the more difficult route? They argue that answering this question, understanding the attraction of such transnational adoptions, is possible only when we look at the two processes together and understand that each fits into the larger American social landscape. They demonstrate that parents' choice to adopt from Romania reflects many American social values and norms, including the ways that Americans see poverty differently in the United States and in a poor country such as Romania. Romanian children are seen as "savable," needing rescue, innocent, and without extra baggage. The children in the American foster system, on the other hand, are seen as "damaged goods." Usually coming from poor families within the United States, children in the U.S. foster system are seen as carrying all the baggage that is presumed about the American poor: that there is something "intrinsically pathological and completely irredeemable" (Ortiz and Briggs 2003:40) about them. At least implicitly, these patterns of adoption suggest that many Americans assume that intervention might work in the case of poor innocent children from overseas but not in the case of children from the domestic foster system.

Sara Dorow (2006b) comes to similar conclusions in her examination of adoptions from China. She discusses the "white noise" of blackness that pervades many of these adoptions, where parents prefer to adopt from China implicitly or even explicitly because the children are not black (Dorow 2006b:210ff; see also Kim 2008). Here, discourses of racial inequality and available forms of adoption within the United States collide with the social, political, and economic constraints on families and adoption within another country. One result is that foreign children are seen as able to be rescued in a way that poor American children—particularly poor black American children—are not. In addition, many parents believe that Chinese adoptees can arrive with "clean slates" and adopting parents will not have to deal with the messy business of birth parents who may want some determined or undetermined future relationship (Dorow 2006b). That is often true, in fact; open adoption records mean that birth parents and children in the United States may develop a relationship. Adoptive parents may initially resist this threat to creating an "as if" biological family, although many parents eventually learn that not having knowledge of birth parents may make the adoption and the child's adjustment and search for connections and identity more difficult later in their lives.

These perspectives remind us just how complex adoption is. Adoptions in the United States invariably cross lines—of color, nationality, race, ethnicity, religion, and socioeconomic class, among others. When individuals cross those lines, when they disrupt assumptions of the normal boundaries between groups or challenge notions of singular and essential identity, they have to deal with sometimes difficult consequences. Individuals who cross these boundaries, through adoption or other means, may come to appreciate the richness of the lives and identities they move among and come to recognize the value of multiple subjectivities.

When we listen to adoptees, those adopted within the United States and those adopted from other countries, we see how complex these adoptions and subsequent family experiences can be. Adoptions today frequently cross lines of race and ethnicity, even in those cases in which it is other borders— such as national borders, in the case of transnational adoption—that draw most attention. The ways that many adopted children and their families and communities must deal explicitly with issues of race reveal many of the social and cultural lines that divide our societies, lines that often go unnoticed until they are crossed. In an interview with researchers Rita Simon and Rhona Roorda (2000), Donna discusses what it meant to be a black child growing up in her adoptive white family in the 1970s and the advantages and challenges that produced. She reports,

> My family has provided me with a resource. Race has been hypersensitized in our home. I have discussions on race that I don't think a lot of people have in their homes. They have to go to school to take a class on race whereas it was a reality in my home. We learned to deal with it and freely discuss it. We don't always agree, but we are comfortable in expressing our opinions. (Simon and Roorda 2000:39)

She continues this theme later in the interview, when she explains that as an adult she identifies as black and that most of her friends are black and explains how her self-identity developed in the midst of a white family:

> I did not take my blackness for granted as many black people do. They don't think about greens and cornbread, about how they raise their families or socialize, about how they walk and talk. I never took blackness for granted because I was the opposite of everyone related to me. I had a heightened awareness of my blackness. I never had a problem being black and never wished I was white. (Simon and Roorda 2000:37).

In these ways, Donna's family and adoption experiences were obviously central to the development of her own ideas about race, and the efforts of her white adoptive parents to connect her to black individuals, communities, and issues were, in her mind, successful in helping her to develop a strong black identity.

But she also describes how she and her family experienced many incidents of racism, receiving hate mail and having a burning cross placed on their front lawn. Clearly, her notions of race were also influenced by what happened outside her family; responding to a question about whether race was an issue, she says, "It was definitely an issue because race is an issue in the larger society and I was a black child living in a white family—so race was an issue" (Simon and Roorda 2000:35). When asked directly about transracial adoption, she says that she believes that "a black child should, if possible, be placed with a black family" but concedes that she would rather have a child "with a family who loves the child rather than in foster care" (Simon and Roorda 2000:38). Donna emphasizes the need for white families to expose black children to their "own culture" (Simon and Roorda 2000:38), just as others argue for the need to provide black children with strategies for dealing with the realities of racism. Although Donna's views are certainly not the only ones voiced among transracial or transnational adoptees, Donna's experiences highlight the ways that white families—and the communities around them—are challenged to deal directly and explicitly with "the hard nut of race" (Rothman 2005:88), the social construction of identity, and the process of making a family in ways that they might not have otherwise.

Socioeconomic class and poverty are also key elements in adoption, and here too, adoption raises issues well beyond adoption. We know that poverty is central to the relinquishing or removal of children in the United States. (Remember, in Norway, where government economic support of children and families is strong, nearly no children are relinquished.) Given that, how do we reconcile the number of children in foster care with our commitment to the best interests of the child? How do we attend to the needs of foster children in our country in ways that support birth parents, foster parents, potential adopting parents, and the children themselves? Is it better for children to remain with their birth parents, perhaps with government aid, than to be raised in another setting?

Similar complexities are present in transnational adoption. Ethiopia exemplifies the ambiguity of these processes. Because of war and disease, especially HIV/AIDS, Ethiopia struggles to provide for nearly 5 million orphans ("Strained by AIDS Orphans" 2004). One of the world's poorest countries, Ethiopia is struggling to deal with this burden, among many others. Partly to ease that burden, the Ethiopian government has begun to welcome foreign adoptions. Foreign adoption agencies have been instrumental in helping Ethiopia set up a system to handle foreign adoptions (including transitional foster homes for future adoptees), and some children are now able to find permanent stable homes because of these new programs. At the same time, some Ethiopian officials worry that while outside help has made a difference, the country may not be quite ready to handle a large number of such adoptions (Gross and Connors 2007). Other officials recognize that these foreign adoptions, while helping to relieve some economic pressures in caring for orphaned children, do not solve the major problems. One official admitted, "Adoption is the last resort because it doesn't help allevi- ate poverty in Ethiopia" ("Strained by AIDS Orphans" 2004). Transnational adoption certainly solves several needs at once—finding homes for children without them and finding children for parents who often are desperate to have children—but it does not deal with the underlying issues that lead to the large numbers of orphaned and abandoned children, including poverty, disease, and war.

In this book we have also shown that as often as adoption efforts are directed toward making as if (biological) families, adoption and fostering also signal an acceptance of new and diverse family forms. In 2008, *The New York Times* ran a story (Winerip 2008) that illustrates how adoption can help to structure a family. When Moriah, a 19-year-old woman, became pregnant, she decided that she wanted to bear her child and find adopting parents to raise him. She began to search for adoptive parents who she thought would fit with her own ideas of a good adoption: parents who would allow her continued contact with her child, even as the child would be theirs. She found such parents in Liane and Kerry, who lived in another state. This couple believed that such an adoption—one that was not only open but allowed the birth mother a place in the child's life—was best for the child. In this family, certainly one configured differently than the closed adoptions promoted in the United States several decades ago, the birth parents and their own families have a relationship and regular visits with the adopting parents and the child. Because of the deliberate efforts of everyone involved, the child, Phelan (whose name was chosen by both birth and adopting parents), has a large kin network with which he spends regular time.

While this kind of adoption is not for everyone, it does suggest how adoption has helped to create diverse family forms in the United States and just how families—all families—are produced and created through the efforts of people. Adoption, of course, is not the only way this has happened.

High divorce rates, along with a high rate of remarriage, has made "blended" families common in most communities; never-married single parents are also now an increasing percentage of parents in any community. Adoption is another set of practices for "doing" family or making families: Adoption has allowed people who would otherwise not have had an opportunity to be parents to create families. And it is this lesson that is perhaps the most obvious lesson to be learned from adoption: the ways that families are socially constructed. What we might think of as a natural grouping of people in a family becomes, after studying adoption, clearly a group that works at doing family. As we have seen, even with no biological or genetic connections, adoptive families resemble other families in how members associate with and care for one another. These similarities underscore that it is not necessary for families to have biological ties to be constructed or maintained. On the other hand, as we look at how people and authorities have handled adoption—who is allowed to adopt and who is not, which children are adopted by which parents—we see that in the United States, we continue to look to biology for our models of the best families. Adoption may reinforce that model as adoptive families strive to be like "regular" families and as states intervene in the definition and structuring of families. At the same time, adoption also challenges the biological model because of all the ways that adoptive families are clearly "normal families" yet at the same time sometimes visibly unlike birth families. Adoption is thus a crucial part of social life in the twenty-first century, allowing alternative pathways for constructing families and challenging us to reflect on and renovate our conceptions of family, society, and self into the future.

Bibliography

Adamec, C. and W. L. Pierce. 2000. *The Encyclopedia of Adoption.* New York: Facts on File.

Aizenman, N. C. and Manuel Roig-Franzia. 2007. "Would-be Parents Fret over Looming Changes; Guatemala Expected to Revise Adoption System." *The Washington Post,* December 1, p. B01.

Alber, Erdmute. 2003. "Denying Biological Parenthood: Fosterage in Northern Benin." *Ethnos* 68(4):487–506.

Alber, Erdmute. 2004a. "Grandparents as Foster Parents: Transformations in Foster Relations between Grandparents and Grandchildren in Northern Benin." *Africa* 74(1):28–46.

Alber, Erdmute. 2004b. "'The Real Parents Are the Foster Parents': Social Parenthood among the Baatombu in Northern Benin." Pp. 33–47 in *Cross Cultural Approaches to Adoption,* edited by F. Bowie. London: Routledge.

Alstein, H. and R. J. Simon, eds. 1990. *Intercountry Adoption: A Multinational Perspective.* New York: Praeger.

Anagnost, Ann. 2000. "Scenes of Misrecognition: Maternal Citizenship in the Age of Transnational Adoption." *positions* 8(2):389–428.

Appadurai, Arjun. 1991. "Global Ethnoscapes: Notes and Queries for a Transnational Anthropology." Pp. 191–210 in *Recapturing Anthropology: Working in the Present,* edited by R. Fox. Santa Fe, NM: School of American Research.

Aries, Philippe. 1962. *Centuries of Childhood: A Social History of Family Life.* New York: Vintage.

Arnold, Denise and Juan de Dios Yapita. 1996. "Los caminos de género en Qaqachaka: Saberes femeninos y discursos textuales alternativos en los Andes." Pp. 303–92 in *Ser mujer indígena, chola, o birlocha en la Bolivia poscolonial de los años 90,* edited by S. R. Cusicanqui. La Paz, Bolivia: Hisbol/Instituto de Langu y Cultura Aymara.

Atwood, Thomas, Lee Allen, Virginia Ravenel, and Nicole Callahan, eds. 2007. *Adoption Factbook IV.* Alexandria, VA: National Council for Adoption.

Bachrach, Christine. 1983. "Adoption as a Means of Family Formation: Data from the National Survey of Family Growth." *Journal of Marriage and Family* 45(4):859–65.

Bachrach, Christine. 1986. "Adoption Plans, Adopted Children, and Adoptive Mothers." *Journal of Marriage and Family* 48(2):243–53.

Bachrach, Christine A., Kathryn A. London, and Penelope L. Maza. 1991. "On the Path to Adoption: Adoption Seeking in the United States, 1988." *Journal of Marriage and Family* 53(3):705–18.

Balcom, Karen. 2006. "Constructing Families, Creating Mothers: Gender, Family, State and Nation in the History of Child Adoption." *Journal of Women's History* 18(1):219–32.

Barry, Ellen. 2007. "A Marketing Campaign from One Heart to Another." *The New York Times,* August 22, p. B2.

Bartholet, Elizabeth. 1999. *Nobody's Children: Abuse and Neglect, Foster Drift, and the Adoption Alternative.* Boston, MA: Beacon.

Berebitsky, Julie. 2000. *Like Our Very Own: Adoption and the Changing Culture of Motherhood, 1851–1950.* Lawrence: University of Kansas Press.

Billingsley, Andrew and Jeanne Giovannoni. 1972. *Children of the Storm: Black Children and American Child Welfare.* New York: Harcourt, Brace, Jovanovich.

Bledsoe, Caroline. 1990a. "'No Success without Struggle': Social Mobility and Hardship for Foster Children in Sierra Leone." *Man* 25(1):70–88.

Bledsoe, Caroline. 1990b. "The Politics of Children: Fosterage and the Social Management of Fertility among the Mende of Sierra Leone." Pp. 81–100 in *Births and Power: Social Change and the Politics of Reproduction,* edited by W. P. Handwerker. Boulder, CO: Westview.

Bledsoe, Caroline. 1993. "Politics of Polygyny in Mende Education and Child Fosterage Transactions." Pp. 170–92 in *Sex and Gender Hierarchies,* edited by B. D. Miller. Cambridge, UK: Cambridge University Press.

Bradley, Carla and Cynthia Hawkins-Leon. 2002. "The Transracial Adoption Debate: Counseling and Legal Implications." *Journal of Counseling and Development* 80(4):433–40.

Briggs, Laura. 2003. "Mother, Child, Race, Nation: The Visual Iconography of Rescue and the Politics of Transnational and Transracial Adoption." *Gender & History* 15(2003):179–200.

Briggs, Laura. 2006a. "Making 'American' Families: Transnational Adoption and U.S. Latin America Policy." Pp. 344–65 in *Haunted by Empire: Geographies of Empire in North American History,* edited by A. L. Stoler. Durham, NC: Duke University Press.

Briggs, Laura. 2006b. "Orphaning the Children of Welfare: 'Crack Babies,' Race, and Adoption Reform." Pp. 75–88 in *Outsiders Within: Racial Crossings and Adoption Politics,* edited by J. J. Trenka, J. C. Oparah, and S. Y. Shin. Boston, MA: South End.

Brown, Caroline and Lisa Rieger. 2001. "Culture and Compliance: Locating the Indian Child Welfare Act in Practice." *Political and Legal Anthropology Review* 24(2):58–75.

Carp, E. Wayne. 1998. *Family Matters: Secrecy and Disclosure in the History of Adoption.* Cambridge, MA: Harvard University Press.

Carroll, Vern, ed. 1970. *Adoption in East Oceania.* Honolulu: University of Hawai'i Press.

Carsten, Janet, ed. 2000. *Cultures of Relatedness: New Approaches to the Study of Kinship.* Cambridge, UK: Cambridge University Press.

Case, Anne, Christina Paxson, and Joseph Ableidinger. 2004. "Orphans in Africa: Parental Death, Poverty, and School Enrollment." *Demography* 41(3):483–508.

Coontz, Stephanie. 1992. *The Way We Never Were.* New York: Basic Books.

Crischlow, W. 2002. "Western Colonization as Disease: Native Adoption and Cultural Genocide." *Critical Social Work* 2(2):104–27.

Dave Thomas Foundation for Adoption. 2007. "National Foster Care Adoption Attitudes Survey." Retrieved February 11, 2011 (http://www.davethomasfoun dationforadoption.org/AdoptionAttitudeSurvey2007.asp).

Delaney, Carol. 1991. *The Seed and the Soil: Gender and Cosmology in a Turkish Village.* Berkeley: University of California Press.

Dickens, Jonathan. 2002. "The Paradox of Inter-country Adoption: Analysing Romania's Experience as a Sending Country." *International Journal of Social Welfare* 11(1):76–83.

Dorow, Sara. 2002. "China Я Us? Care, Consumption, and Transnationally Adopted Children." Pp. 149–68 in *Symbolic Childhood,* edited by D. Cook. New York: Peter Lang.

Dorow, Sara. 2006a. "Racialized Choices: Chinese Adoption and the 'White Noise' of Blackness." *Critical Sociology* 32(2/3):357–79.

Dorow, Sara. 2006b. *Transnational Adoption: A Cultural Economy of Race, Gender, and Kinship.* New York: New York University Press.

Eng, David. 2003. "Transnational Adoption and Queer Diasporas." *Social Text 76* 21(3):1–37.

Fanshel, David. 1972. *Far from the Reservation: The Transracial Adoption of American Indian Children.* Metuchen, NJ: Scarecrow.

Fessler, Anne. 2003. "Everlasting: An Art Installation Representing the Voices of Women Who Surrendered Their Newborns between the Years 1945 and 1973." Retrieved February 4, 2011 (https://danube.mica.edu/backoffice/everlasting/hardhat/menu.html).

Fessler, Anne. 2007. *The Girls Who Went Away: The Hidden History of Women Who Surrendered Children for Adoption in the Decades before Roe v. Wade.* New York: Penguin.

Fogg-Davis, Hawley. 2002. *The Ethics of Transracial Adoption.* Ithaca, NY: Cornell University Press.

Fonseca, Claudia. 1986. "Orphanages, Foundlings, and Foster Mothers: The System of Child Circulation in a Brazilian Squatter Settlement." *Anthropological Quarterly* 59:15–27.

Fonseca, Claudia. 2002. "Inequality Near and Far: Adoption as Seen from the Brazilian Favelas." *Law and Society Review* 36(2):397–432 .

Fonseca, Claudia. 2003. "Patterns of Shared Parenthood among the Brazilian Poor." *Social Text 74: Transnational Adoption* 21(1):111–27.

Fourner, Susanne and Ernie Crey. 1997. *Stolen from Our Embrace: The Abduction of First Nations' Children and the Restoration of Aboriginal Communities.* Toronto, Canada: Douglas and McIntyre.

Frankenberg, Ruth. 1993. *White Women, Race Matters: The Social Construction of Whiteness.* Minneapolis: University of Minnesota Press.

Freundlich, Madelyn and Joy Kim Lieberthal. 2000. "The Gathering of the First Generation of Adult Korean Adoptees: Adoptees' Perceptions of International Adoption." Retrieved August 10, 2009 (http://www.adoptioninstitute.org/proed/korfindings.html).

Gailey, Christine. 1999. "Seeking Baby Right: Race, Class and Gender in U.S. International Adoption." Pp. 52–80 in *Mine, Yours, Ours . . . and Theirs: Adoption Changing Kinship and Family Patterns,* edited by A.-L. Rygvold, M. Dalen, and B. Saetersdal. Oslo, Norway: University of Oslo Press.

Gailey, Christine. 2000a. "Ideologies of Motherhood and Kinship in U.S. Adoption." Pp. 11–55 in *Ideologies and Technologies of Motherhood,* edited by H. Ragoné and F. W. Twine. New York: Routledge.

Gailey, Christine. 2000b. "Race, Class and Gender in Intercountry Adoption in the USA." Pp. 295–314 in *Intercountry Adoption: Development, Trends, and Perspectives,* edited by P. Selman. London: BAAF.

Gale, Lacey Andrews. 2008. *Beyond* men pikin: *Improving Understanding of Post-conflict Child Fostering in Sierra Leone.* Medford, MA: Feinstein International Center, Tufts University. Retrieved May 13, 2010 (https://wikis.uit.tufts.edu/confluence/display/FIC/Beyond+men+pikin).

Gibson, Dawn. 2006. "Childless Adopt Overseas Approach to Parenthood." *The West Australian* (Perth), December 14, p. 50.

Gill, Brian P. 2002. "Adoption Agencies and the Search for the Ideal Family, 1918–1965." Pp. 160–80 in *Adoption in America: Historical Perspectives,* edited by E. W. Carp. Ann Arbor: University of Michigan Press.

Goody, Esther. 1982. *Parenthood and Social Reproduction: Fostering and Occupational Roles in West Africa.* New York: Cambridge University Press.

Gordon, Linda. 1990. *Woman's Body, Woman's Right: Birth Control in America.* New York: Penguin.

Gordon, Linda. 1999. *The Great Arizona Orphan Abduction.* Cambridge, MA: Harvard University Press.

Greenhalgh, Susan and Jiali Li. 1995. "Engendering Reproductive Policy and Practice in Peasant China: For a Feminist Demography of Reproduction." *Signs: Journal of Women in Culture and Society* 20(3):601–41.

Gross, Jane and Will Connors. 2007. "Surge in Adoptions Raises Concern in Ethiopia." *The New York Times,* June 4, p. A1.

Grubb, W. Norton and Marvin Lazerson. [1982] 1988. *Broken Promises: How Americans Fail Their Children.* Chicago, IL: University of Chicago Press.

Hemenway, Robin. 2004. "The Circle of We: The Strange History of American Adoption." *American Quarterly* 56:183–92.

Herman, Ellen. 2008. *Kinship by Design: A History of Adoption in the Modern United States.* Chicago: University of Chicago Press.

Higginbotham, Elizabeth. 1992. "African-American Women's History and the Metalanguage of Race." *Signs: Journal of Women in Culture and Society* 17(2):251–74.

Howell, Signe. 2001. "Self-conscious Kinship: Some Contested Values in Norwegian Transnational Adoption." Pp. 204–23 in *Relative Values,* edited by S. Franklin and S. McKinnon. Durham, NC: Duke University Press.

Howell, Signe. 2006. *The Kinning of Foreigners: Transnational Adoption in a Global Perspective.* New York: Berghahn Books.

Howell, Signe and Diana Marre. 2006. "To Kin a Transnationally Adopted Child in Norway and Spain: The Achievement of Resemblances and Belonging." *Ethnos* 71(3):293–316.

Hübinette, Tobias. 2006. "From Orphan Trains to Babylifts: Colonial Trafficking, Empire Building, and Social Engineering." Pp. 139–49 in *Outsiders Within: Writing on Transracial Adoption,* edited by J. J. Trenka, J. C. Oparah, and S. Y. Shin. Cambridge, MA: South End.

Hübinette, Tobias. 2007. "Nationalism, Subalternity, and the Adopted Koreans." *Journal of Women's History* 19(1):117–22.

Inhorn, Marcia. 1996. *Infertility and Patriarchy: The Cultural Politics of Gender and Family Life in Egypt.* Philadelphia: University of Pennsylvania Press.

Inhorn, Marcia. 2006. "'He Won't Be My Son': Middle Eastern Muslim Men's Discourses of Adoption and Gamete Donation." *Medical Anthropology Quarterly* 20(1):94–120.

Ionescu, Camiola. 2005. "Romania's Abandoned Children Are Still Suffering." *Lancet* 366:1595–96.

Jacobsen, Heather. 2008. *Culture Keeping: White Mothers, International Adoption and the Negotiation of Family Difference.* Nashville, TN: Vanderbilt University Press.

Jaffe, E., ed. 1995. *Intercountry Adoptions: Laws and Perspectives of "Sending" Countries.* London: Martinus Nijhoff.

Johnson, Kay. 2002. "Politics of International and Domestic Adoption in China." *Law and Society Review* 36(2):379–96.

Johnson, Mary Ellen, comp., and Kay B. Hall, ed. 1992. *Orphan Train Riders: Their Own Stories.* Baltimore, MD: Gateway Press.

Kahan, Michelle. 2006. "'Put up' on Platforms: A History of Twentieth Century Adoption Policy in the United States." *Journal of Sociology and Social Welfare* 33(3):51–72.

Kane, Saralee. "The Movement of Children for International Adoption: An Epidemiological Perspective." *Social Science Journal* 30(4):323–40.

Kasimitz, Philip. 2007. "Thoughts on *My Homeland Décor.*" *Qualitative Sociology* 30:221–24.

Kennedy, Randall. 2003. *Interracial Intimacies: Sex, Marriage, Identity, and Adoption.* New York: Pantheon.

Kim, Eleana. 2007. "Transnational Adoption: A Cultural Economy of Race, Gender, and Kinship." *Anthropological Quarterly* 80(2):589–96.

Kim, Katherin. 2008. "Out of Sorts: Adoption and (Un)desirable Children." Pp. 393–406 in *Mapping the Social Landscape,* edited by S. Ferguson. Boston, MA: McGraw-Hill.

Kingsolver, Barbara. 1993. *Pigs in Heaven.* New York: HarperCollins.

Klein, Christina. 2003. *Cold War Orientalism: Asia in the Middlebrow Imagination, 1945–1961.* Berkeley: University of California Press.

Kligman, Gail. 1992. "Abortion and International Adoption in Post-Ceausescu Romania." *Feminist Studies* 18(2):405–19.

Kohler, Julie K., Harold D. Grotevant, and Ruth G. McRoy. 2002. "Adopted Adolescents' Preoccupation with Adoption: The Impact on Adoptive Family Relationships." *Journal of Marriage and Family* 64(1):93–104.

Krieder, Rose. 2007. "Adoptive Children and Stepchildren: Census 2000 Special Reports." Pp. 133–54 in *Adoption Factbook IV,* edited by T. Atwood, L. Allen, V. Ravenel, and N. Callahan. Alexandria, VA: National Council for Adoption.

Laffan, Grainger. 2005. "Romania's Policy of Emptying Its Orphanages Raises Controversy." *British Medical Journal* 331:1360.

Lee, Bong Joo. 2007. "Adoption in Korea: Current Status and Future Prospects." *International Journal of Social Welfare* 16:75–83.

Lee, Robert G. 1999. *Orientals: Asian Americans in Popular Culture.* Philadelphia: Temple University Press.

Leinaweaver, Jessaca. 2005. "Accompanying and Overcoming: Subsistence and Sustenance in an Andean City." *Michigan Discussions in Anthropology* 15:150–82.

Leinaweaver, Jessaca. 2007. "On Moving Children: The Social Implications of Andean Child Circulation." *American Ethnologist* 34(1):163–80.

Leinaweaver, Jessaca. 2008. *The Circulation of Children: Kinship, Adoption, and Morality in Andean Peru.* Durham, NC: Duke University Press.

Lo, Beth Kyong. 2006. "Korean Psych 101: Concepts of Hwa-Byung in Relation to Korean Adoption." Pp. 167–76 in *Outsiders Within: Writing on Transracial Adoption,* edited by J. J. Trenka, J. C. Oparah, and S. Y. Shin. Cambridge, MA: South End.

Lovelock, Kirsten. 2000. "Intercountry Adoption as a Migratory Practice: A Comparative Analysis of Intercountry Adoption and Immigration Policy and Practice in the United States, Canada and New Zealand in the Post WWII Period." *International Migration Review* 34(3):907–49.

Luke, Carmen and Allan Luke. 1998. "Interracial Families: Difference within Difference." *Ethnic and Racial Studies* 21:728–53.

MacDonald, Nancy and Judy MacDonald. 2007. "Reflections of a Mi'kmaq Social Worker on a Quarter of a Century Work in First Nations Child Welfare." *First Peoples Child and Family Review* 3(1):34–45.

Manzo, Kathryn. 1996. *Creating Boundaries: The Politics of Race and Nation.* Boulder, CO: Lynne Rienner.

March, Karen. 1995. "Perception of Adoption as Social Stigma: Motivation for Search and Reunion." *Journal of Marriage and Family* 57(3):653–60.

May, Elaine Tyler. 1995. *Barren in the Promised Land: Childless Americans and the Pursuit of Happiness.* Cambridge, MA: Harvard University Press.

McCabe, Nancy. 2003. *Meeting Sophie: A Memoir of Adoption*. Columbia: University of Missouri Press.

McLanahan, Sara and Gary Sandefur. 1994. *Growing up with a Single Parent: What Hurts, What Helps*. Cambridge, MA: Harvard University Press.

Melosh, Barbara. 2002. *Strangers and Kin: The American Way of Adoption*. Cambridge, MA: Harvard University Press.

Menozzi, Claire. 2008. "What Do We Know about Adoption?" Breakfast Seminar by United Nations Population Division presented at the Population Association of America annual meeting, April 17, New Orleans, LA.

Mills, Antonia and Linda Champion. 1996. "Come-backs/Reincarnation as Integration; Adoption-out as Disassociation: Examples from First Nations Northwest British Columbia." *Anthropology of Consciousness* 7(3):30–43.

Mills, C. Wright. 1959. *The Sociological Imagination*. Oxford, UK: Oxford University Press.

Modell, Judith. 1994. *Kinship with Strangers: Adoption and Interpretation of Kinship in American Culture*. Berkeley: University of California Press.

Modell, Judith. 1997. "Rights to Children: Foster Care and Social Reproduction in Hawai'i." Pp. 156–72 in *Reproducing Reproduction: Kinship, Power, and Technological Innovation*, edited by S. Franklin and H. Ragoné. Philadelphia: University of Pennsylvania Press.

Moore, Kristin and Zakia Redd. 2002. "Children in Poverty: Trends, Consequences, and Policy Options." Childtrends Research Brief No. 2002-54. Retrieved January 20, 2010 (www.childtrends.org).

Morris, Rita. 2007. "Voices of Foster Youths: Problems and Ideas for Change." *Urologic Nursing* 27(5):419–27.

Nasr, Seyyed Hossain. [1966] 1985. *Ideas and Realities of Islam*. London: Allen and Unwin.

Nazario, Sonia. 2007. "Negotiating the Difficulties of a Delicate Pact." *Los Angeles Times*, August 9, p. A1.

Nelson, Claudia. 2003. *Little Strangers: Portrayals of Adoption and Foster Care in America, 1850–1929*. Bloomington: Indiana University Press.

Notermans, Catrien. 2004. "Fosterage and the Politics of Marriage and Kinship in East Cameroon." Pp. 48–63 in *Cross Cultural Approaches to Adoption*, edited by F. Bowie. New York: Routledge.

Novey, Marianne, ed. 2001. *Imagining Adoption: Essays on Literature and Culture*. Ann Arbor: University of Michigan Press.

Omi, Michael and Howard Winant. 1994. *Racial Formation in the United States: From the 1960s to the 1990s*. 2nd ed. New York: Routledge.

Ortiz, Ana Teresa and Laura Briggs. 2003. "Culture of Poverty, Crack Babies, and Welfare Cheats." *Social Text* 21(3):39–58.

Patton, Sandra. 2000. *Birth Marks: Transracial Adoption in Contemporary America*. New York: New York University Press.

Pertman, Adam. 2000. *Adoption Nation: How the Adoption Revolution Is Transforming America*. New York: Basic Books.

Pilkington, Doris. 2002. *Rabbit Proof Fence*. New York: Hyperion.

Placek, Paul. 2007. "National Adoption Data." Pp. 3–70 in *Adoption Factbook IV*, edited by T. Atwood, L. Allen, V. Ravenel, and N. Callahan. Alexandria, VA: National Council for Adoption.

Polgreen, Lydia. 2008. "Overcoming Customs and Stigma, Sudan Gives Orphans a Lifeline." *The New York Times*, April 5, p. 6.

Porter, Roy. 1988. "Points of Entry: The Foundling Hospital." *History Today* 38(3):61–63.

Porter, Susan L. 2002. "A Good Home: Indenture and Adoption in Nineteenth–century Orphanages." Pp. 27–50 in *Adoption in America: Historical Perspectives*, edited by E. W. Carp. Ann Arbor: University of Michigan Press.

Rainwater, Lee and Timothy Smeeding. 2003. *Poor Kids in a Rich Country*. New York: Russell Sage.

Riley, Nancy E. 1997. "American Adoptions of Chinese Girls: The Socio-political Matrices of Individual Decisions." *Women's Studies International Forum* 20(1):87–103.

Roberts, Dorothy. 2002. *Shattered Bonds: The Color of Child Welfare*. New York: Basic Books.

Roberts, Dorothy E. 1999. "Poverty, Race, and New Directions in Child Welfare Policy." *Washington University Journal of Law and Policy* 1(63):65–66.

Rothman, Barbara Katz. 2005. *Weaving a Family: Untangling Race and Adoption*. Boston, MA: Beacon.

Schulman, Irving and Richard Behrman. 1993. "Adoption Overview and Major Recommendations." *Future of Children* 3(1):4–16.

Secombe, Karen. 2006. *Families in Poverty*. Boston, MA: Allyn & Bacon.

Selman, Peter. 2002. "Intercountry Adoption in the New Millenium: The 'Quiet' Migration Revisited." *Population Research & Policy Review* 21:205–25.

Selman, Peter. 2006. "Trends in Intercountry Adoption 1998–2004: A Demographic Analysis of Data from 20 Receiving States." *Journal of Population Research* 23(2):183–204.

Simon, Rita J. and Howard Altstein. [1992] 2002. *Adoption, Race, and Identity: From Infancy to Young Adulthood*. 2nd ed. New Brunswick, NJ: Transaction Publishing.

Simon, Rita J. and Sarah Hernandez. 2008. *Native American Transracial Adoptees Tell Their Stories*. Lanham, MD: Lexington Books.

Simon, Rita and Rhona Roorda. 2000. *In Their Own Voices: Transracial Adoptees Tell Their Stories*. New York: Columbia University Press.

Snow, Rebekah and Katherine Covell. 2006. "Adoption and the Best Interests of the Child: The Dilemma of Cultural Interpretation." *International Journal of Children's Rights* 14:109–17.

Sobol, Michael P. and Kerry J. Daly. 1994. "Canadian Adoption Statistics: 1981–1990." *Journal of Marriage and Family* 56(2):493–99.

Solinger, Rickie. 2001. *Beggars and Choosers: How the Politics of Choice Shapes Adoption, Abortion, and Welfare in the United States*. New York: Hill and Wang.

Spivak, Gayatri Chakravorty. 1993. *Outside in the Teaching Machine*. New York: Routledge.

Stacey, Judith and Timothy Biblarz. 2001. "(How) Does the Sexual Orientation of Parents Matter?" *American Sociological Review* 66(2):159–83.

Stack, Carol. 1974. *All Our Kin*. New York: Basic Books.

Stack, Carol. 1996. *Call to Home: African Americans Reclaim the Rural South*. New York: Basic Books.

Stark, Heidi Kiiwetinepinesiik and Kekek Jason Todd Stark. 2006. "Flying the Coop: ICWA and the Welfare of Indian Children." Pp.125–38 in *Outsiders Within: Writing on Transracial Adoption*, edited by J. J. Trenka, J. C. Oparah, and S. Y. Shin. Cambridge, MA: South End.

Steinberg, Gail and Beth Hall. 2000. *Inside Transracial Adoption*. Indianapolis, IN: Perspectives Press.

Stoler, Ann. 1989. "Making Empire Respectable: The Politics of Race and Sexual Morality in 20th Century Colonial Cultures." *American Ethnologist* 16(4):634–60.

"Strained by AIDS Orphans, Ethiopia Eases Adoptions by Foreigners." 2004. *The New York Times*, December 26, p 1.15.

Strong, Pauline Turner and Barrik Van Winkle. 1996. "'Indian Blood': Reflections on the Reckoning and Refiguring of Native North American Identity." *Cultural Anthropology* 11(4):547–76.

Tessler, Richard, Gail Gamache, and Liming Liu. 1999. *West Meets East: Americans Adopt Chinese Children*. Westport, CT: Bergin and Garvey.

Traver, Amy. 2007. "Home(land) Décor: China Adoptive Parents' Consumption of Chinese Cultural Objects for Display in Their Homes." *Qualitative Sociology* 30:201–20.

Trenka, Jane Jeong, Julia Chinyere Oparah, and SunYung Shin, eds. 2006. *Outsiders Within: Racial Crossings and Adoption Politics*. Cambridge, MA: South End.

Uhlenberg, Peter. 1980. "Death and the Family." *Journal of Family History* 5(3):313–20.

UNAIDS, UNICEF, and USAID. 2004. *Children on the Brink: A Joint Report of New Orphan Estimates and a Framework for Action*. Washington, DC: USAID.

Unger, Steven, ed. 1977. *The Destruction of American Indian Families*. New York: Association on American Indian Affairs.

UNICEF. 2003. *Africa's Orphaned Generations*. New York: UNICEF. Retrieved January 31, 2011 (www.unicef.org/sowc06/pdfs/africas_orphans.pdf).

United Nations Population Division. 2009. *Child Adoption: Trends and Policies*. New York: United Nations.

Upton, Rebecca L. 2003. "'Women Have No Tribe': Connecting Carework, Gender, and Migration in an Era of HIV/AIDS in Botswana." *Gender & Society* 17(2):314–22.

U.S. Department of Health and Human Services, Children's Bureau. 2008. "Trends in Foster Care and Adoption: 2007–8." Retrieved April 14, 2009 (http://www.acf.hhs.gov/programs/cb/stats_research/afcars/trends.htm).

Van Vleet, Krista E. 2002. "The Intimacies of Power: Rethinking Violence and Affinity in the Bolivian Andes." *American Ethnologist* 29(3):567–601.

Van Vleet, Krista E. 2008. *Performing Kinship: Narrative, Gender, and the Intimacies of Power in the Andes*. Austin: University of Texas Press.

Vance, Carole. [1991] 2005. "Anthropology Rediscovers Sexuality: A Theoretical Comment." Pp. 14–32 in *Same Sex Cultures and Sexualities: An Anthropological Reader,* edited by J. Robertson. New York: John Wiley.

Verhoef, Heidi. 2005. "A Child Has Many Mothers: Views of Child Fostering in Northwestern Cameroon." *Childhood* 12:369–90.

Verhoef, Heidi and Gilda Morelli. 2007. "'A Child Is a Child': Fostering Experiences in Northwestern Cameroon." *Ethos* 35(1):33–64.

Volkman, Toby. 2005. "Embodying Chinese Culture: Transnational Adoption in America." Pp. 81–113 in *Cultures of Transnational Adoption,* edited by T. Volkman. Durham, NC: Duke University Press.

Wade, Peter. 1997. *Race and Ethnicity in Latin America.* New York: Pluto.

Walmsley, Emily. 2008. "Raised by Another Mother: Informal Fostering and Kinship Ambiguities in Northwest Ecuador." *Journal of Latin American and Caribbean Anthropology* 13(1):168–95.

Weismantel, Mary. 1995. "Making Kin: Kinship Theory and Zumbagua Adoptions." *American Ethnologist* 22(4):685–709.

Williams, Patricia. 1991. *The Alchemy of Race and Rights.* Cambridge, MA: Harvard University Press.

Wilson, Samantha and Judith Gibbons. 2005. "Guatemalan Perceptions of Adoption." *International Social Work* 48(6):742–52.

Winerip, Michael. 2008. "With Open Adoption, a New Kind of Family." *The New York Times,* February 24, p. L1.4.

Wright, Jeni. 2006. "Love Is Colorblind: Reflections of a Mixed Girl." Pp. 27–30 in *Outsiders Within: Writing on Transracial Adoption,* edited by J. J. Trenka, J. C. Oparah, and S. Y. Shin. Cambridge, MA: South End.

Wu, Frank. 2003. *Yellow: Race in America beyond Black and White.* New York: Basic Books.

Yanagisako, Sylvia and Carole Delaney. 1995. "Naturalizing Power." Pp. 1–24 in *Naturalizing Power,* edited by S. Yanagisako and C. Delaney. New York: Routledge.

Yngvesson, Barbara. 1997. "Negotiating Motherhood: Identity and Difference in 'Open' Adoption." *Law and Society Review* 31:31–80.

Yngvesson, Barbara. 2000. "'Un Niño de Cualquier Color': Race and Nation in Intercountry Adoption." Pp. 247–305 in *Globalizing Institutions: Case Studies in Regulation and Innovation,* edited by J. Jenson and B. de Sousa Santos. Aldershot, UK: Ashgate.

Yngvesson, Barbara. 2002. "Placing the 'Gift Child' in Transnational Adoption." *Law and Society Review* 36(2):227–56.

Yngvesson, Barbara. 2005. "Going 'Home': Adoption, Loss of Bearings, and the Mythology of Roots." Pp. 25–48 in *Cultures of Transnational Adoption,* edited by T. Volkman. Durham, NC: Duke University Press.

Yngvesson, Barbara and Susan Bibler Coutin. 2006. "Backed by Papers: Undoing Persons, Histories, and Return." *American Ethnologist* 33(2):177–90.

Zelizer, Viviana. 1995. *Pricing the Priceless Child.* Princeton, NJ: Princeton University Press.

Zhang Weiguo. 2006. "Child Adoption in Contemporary Rural China." *Journal of Family Issues* 27(3):301–40.

Websites Consulted

- Adoption History Project, University of Oregon: http://darkwing.uoregon.edu/~adoption/
- Families with Children from China: www.fwcc.org
- http://www.acf.hhs.gov/programs/cb/stats_research/afcars/trends.htm
- http://www.lambdalegal.org
- http://www.travel.state.gov/family/adoption/stats/stats_451.html
- International Korean Adoption Service (InKAS): http://www.inkas.or.kr/
- National Adoption Information Clearinghouse: http://www.adoption.org/adopt/national-adoption-clearinghouse.php
- National Council for Adoption: https://www.adoptioncouncil.org
- On adoptions from Romania: http://romania.adoption.com
- On U.S. foster care: http://www. childwelfare.gov
- One World, a website for adoptees from China: http://www.chineseadoptee.com/
- Statistics Norway: http://www.ssb.no/adopsjon_en/
- U.S. State Department, Intercountry Adoption, Office of Children Issues: http://adoption.state.gov/

Further Exploration

We present a range of materials about adoption that readers may find useful. This is just a selection of the myriad of materials available.

Movies (Full-Length)

Casa de los Babys. 2003. Director: John Sayles.

Six American women, who are in a(n) (unnamed) Latin American country to adopt babies, discuss issues of motherhood, adoption, and relationships between the United States and other countries.

Juno. 2007. Director: Jason Reitman.

Juno, a 16-year-old pregnant woman, decides to continue her pregnancy and place her child with an adopting family whom she chooses and gets to know during the pregnancy.

*Losing Isaiah.*1995. Director: Stephen Gyllenhaal.

A white social worker adopts a child abandoned by a mother addicted to crack. Years later the black birthmother finds out that her son is not dead as she thought and goes to court to get him back.

Mother and Child. 2010. **Director: Rodrigo García.**

Three women whose lives have been shaped by adoption: Karen had a baby at 14 and gave her up at birth; Elizabeth grew up an adopted child; and Lucy looks for a baby to adopt.

Rabbit Proof Fence. 2002. Director: Phillip Noyce.

This film is set in western Australia. Three half-aboriginal children are removed from their mother by the government and sent across the country to be "reformed" and socialized into white society. This is the story of their ordeal in the boarding school and effort to return to their mother.

Secrets and Lies. 1996. Director: Mike Leigh.

A successful black woman traces her birth mother and finds that she is white. The developing relationship reveals "secrets and lies" found in many families.

Then She Found Me. 2007. Director: Helen Hunt.

A schoolteacher in New York deals with several crises at once as her husband leaves, her adoptive mother dies, and her birth mother appears.

Documentaries

China's Lost Girls. 2004. (National Geographic).

This film follows a group of American parents to China where they adopt daughters.

Goodbye Baby. 2005. Director: Patricia Goudvis (New Day Films).

This film is about the growing practice of U.S. citizens' adopting Guatemalan children. It presents perspectives of Guatemalans as well as adoptive parents about this practice.

First Person Plural. 2000. Deann Borshay Liem (Independent Television Service, PBS).

A Korean adoptee traces her Korean roots and wrestles with her identities as American, Korean, and daughter.

Websites

Adoption History Project, University of Oregon: http://www.uoregon.edu/~adoption/

This website covers a range of topics in the history of adoption in the United States.

Hague Convention on Protection of Children and Cooperation in Respect of Intercountry Adoption: http://www.hcch.net/index_en.php?act=conventionstext&cid=69

This site presents the full text of the Hague Convention.

International Korean Adoption Service (InKAS): http://www.inkas.or.kr/

This is a site that serves the needs of Korean adoptees, giving aid in finding birth parents and visiting Korea, among many other activities.

National Adoption Information Clearinghouse: http://www.adoption.org/adopt/national-adoption-clearinghouse.php

This website provides data and information about adoption.

Memoirs and Remembrances

Bensen, Robert, ed. 2001. *Children of the Dragonfly: Native American Voices on Child Custody and Education*. Tucson: University of Arizona Press.

Fessler, Ann. 2007. *The Girls Who Went Away: The Hidden History of Women Who Surrendered Children for Adoption in the Decades before* Roe v. Wade. New York: Penguin.

This is the story of unmarried women who gave up children for adoption before changes in the United States such as birth control, the legalization of abortion, and the acceptance of single motherhood.

Johnson, Mary Ellen, comp., and Kay B. Hall, ed. 1992. *Orphan Train Riders: Their Own Stories*. Baltimore, MD: Gateway Press.

McCabe, Nancy. 2003. *Meeting Sophie: A Memoir of Adoption*. Columbia: University of Missouri Press.

Pilkington, Doris. 1996. *Rabbit Proof Fence*. New York: Hyperion.

The story of how three aboriginal girls, forcibly removed from their families, return home.

Rothman, Barbara Katz. 2005. *Weaving a Family: Untangling Race and Adoption*. Boston, MA: Beacon.

A white sociologist, who is also the adoptive mother of a black daughter, explores the issues of race, family, and motherhood.

Russell, Beth. 2004. *Forever Lily: An Unexpected Mother's Journey to Adoption in China*. New York: Touchstone.

This is the story of an American woman who ends up adopting a child in China only after her friend is unable to care for the child.

Simon, Rita J. and Sarah Hernandez. 2008. *Native American Transracial Adoptees Tell Their Stories*. Lanham, MD: Lexington Books.

Trenka, Jane Jeong. 2003. *The Language of Blood*. St. Paul, MN: Graywolf Press.

This is a memoir of a woman adopted from Korea by white parents in Minnesota. She returns to Korea to meet her Korean mother and siblings.

Trenka, Jane Jeong, Julia Chinyere Oparah, and Sung Yung Shin, eds. 2006. *Outsiders Within: Writing on Transracial Adoption*. Cambridge, MA: South End.

This book contains art, poetry, memoirs, and essays on the challenges of and from transracial adoption.

Fiction

Kingsolver, Barbara. 1993. *Pigs in Heaven*. New York: HarperCollins.

Taylor, a white mother, adopts Turtle, an abandoned Native American girl. We see the difficulties when two separate claims—here an adoptive mother's and the child's Cherokee tribe's—both have some legitimacy.

Lee, Wendy. 2008. *Happy Family*. New York: Grove Press.

This is the story of a Chinese American immigrant who becomes a nanny for a white American family with a child adopted from China.

Patchett, Ann. 2007. *The Patron Saint of Liars*. New York: Perennial.

This novel takes place in a rural home for unmarried mothers. We meet several women who live at the home and come to understand some of the complexities of parenthood.

Tyler, Ann. 2007. *Digging to America*. New York: Ballantine Books.

Over several years, two very different American families—a white American family and an Iranian American family—develop a relationship over their common experience of adopting Korean daughters.

Academic and Policy Treatments of Adoption Issues

Bargach, Jamila. 2002. *Orphans of Islam: Family, Abandonment, and Secret Adoption in Morocco*. Lanham, MD: Rowman & Littlefield.

Brown, Caroline and Lisa Rieger. 2001. "Culture and Compliance: Locating the Indian Child Welfare Act in Practice." *Political and Legal Anthropology Review* 24(2):58–75.

Dorow, Sara. 2006. *Transnational Adoption: A Cultural Economy of Race, Gender, and Kinship*. New York: New York University Press.

Gordon, Linda. 1999. *The Great Arizona Orphan Abduction*. Cambridge, MA: Harvard University Press.

Herman, Ellen. 2008. *Kinship by Design: A History of Adoption in the Modern United States*. Chicago, IL: University of Chicago Press.

Jacobsen, Heather. 2008. *Culture Keeping: White Mothers, International Adoption and the Negotiation of Family Difference*. Nashville, TN: Vanderbilt University Press.

Johnson, Kay. 2004. *Wanting a Daughter, Needing a Son: Abandonment, Adoption, and Orphanage Care in China*. New York: Yeong & Yeong.

This book offers an exploration of how so many girls end up abandoned in China, the role of sons and daughters in Chinese families, and how China's population policies play a role in these issues.

Marre, Diana and Laura Briggs, eds. 2009. *International Adoption: Global Inequalities of the Circulation of Children*. New York: New York University Press.

This is a collection of articles dealing with various aspects of transnational adoption.

Melosh, Barbara. 2002. *Strangers and Kin: The American Way of Adoption*. Cambridge, MA: Harvard University Press.

This is a comprehensive history of adoption in the United States.

Modell, Judith. 2002. *A Sealed and Secret Kinship: The Culture of Policies and Practices in American Adoption*. New York: Berghahn Books.

This book examines issues of adoption such as open and sealed adoption, the search for birth parents, and routes of placement of children for adoption.

Roberts, Dorothy. 2002. *Shattered Bonds: The Color of Child Welfare*. New York: Basic Books.

Legal scholar Roberts examines the disproportionate number of black children in the U.S. foster care system and its effects on black families and communities.

Rothman, Barbara Katz. 2005. *Weaving a Family: Untangling Race and Adoption*. Boston, MA: Beacon.

A white sociologist, who is also the adoptive mother of a black daughter explores the issues of race, family, and motherhood.

Solinger, Rickie. 1992. *Wake up Little Suzie: Single Pregnancy and Race before* Roe v. Wade. New York: Routledge.

This book examines the very different experiences of black and white unmarried women during the period from 1945 to 1965.

Solinger, Rickie. 2001. *Beggars and Choosers: How the Politics of Choice Shapes Adoption, Abortion, and Welfare in the United States*. New York: Hill and Wang.

Solinger traces the meaning and use of *choice* for different groups within the United States and how its use reflects issues of race, class, and gender.

United Nations Population Division. 2009. *Child Adoption: Trends and Policies*. New York: United Nations.

This volume contains adoption statistics and policies for most countries across the world.

Ward Gailey, Christine. 2010. *Blue-ribbon Babies and Labors of Love: Race, Class, and Gender in U.S. Adoptive Practice*. Austin: University of Texas Press.

Special Issues of Journals

2001 *Law and Society Review* 36: "Nonbiological Parenting"
2003 *Social Text* 74: "Transnational Adoption"
2009 *Journal of Latin American and Caribbean Anthropology* 14(1): "Cultural and Political Economies of Transnational Adoption"

Index

Abandoned children, 33, 40, 43, 69–71, 103, 107, 113–115
Abortion, 51, 66, 72, 104, 109
Adopted children's characteristics, 61–62
  adoptable children, 61
  ages, 10–11, 38–39, 42, 88, 127
  special needs, 62, 65, 86
  See also Race and ethnicity
Adoption advocacy organizations, 13
Adoption agencies, 9–10, 44, 47, 49, 51, 58, 63–64, 67, 90, 110, 112
Adoption and Safe Families Act of 1997, 67
Adoption choices, 2
Adoption documentation confidentiality, 46–48, 52
Adoption expenses, 10, 57, 71
  transnational adoption, 106
Adoption information resources:
  academic and policy treatments, 146–147
  bibliography, 132–141
  documentaries, 144
  journal special issues, 147
  literature, 145–147
  movies, 143–144
  sources of adoption statistics, 13
  transnational adoption help, 118
  websites, 118, 142, 144
Adoption in the U.S., historical perspectives, 37–42, 125
  1960s to the present, 50–52
  acceptance of open adoption, 52–53
  attitudes toward single mothers, 43
  child protection, 38–39

documentation secrecy, 46–48
evolution of modern adoption law, 39–41
family form issues, 42–44
orphan trains, 40–41
postwar demand and changing attitudes, 48–50
professionalization and regulation of adoption, 44–47
race and, 77–79
substitute care arrangements, 38
Adoption law and regulation, 44–45, 55–56, 65, 97
  Adoption and Safe Families Act of 1997, 67
  early models, 39–41
  Hague Convention on the Protection of Children, 99–101, 104
  Indian Child Welfare Act, 73, 89–91, 100, 124
  refugee legislation, 101–102
  See also State influence
Adoption statistics, 11–13, 49, 53, 57
Adoption subsidies, 68, 71–72, 106
Adoption terminology, 9–11
Adoptive family visibility, 2, 8, 14, 56, 131
Adoptive parents, 62
  acceptable parents for adoption or fostering, 63–65
  biological versus adoptive parents, 27–29, 43
  matching children's religion or race, 45–46
  private agency criteria for, 10

sexual orientation of, 62–63, 65, 66, 115, 117
socioeconomic class and adoption choices, 57–60
support groups, 118
African Americans:
child-parent matching and, 46
foster placement disparities, 73, 78, 83–85, 92
informal systems of care, 125–126
NABSW statement against transracial adoption, 79–80, 83, 91
See also Race and ethnicity; Transracial adoption
African Charter on Rights and Welfare of the Child, 99–101
AIDS orphans, 35, 129–130
Alber, Erdmute, 16, 30, 34
Andean informal fostering, 21–24, 27–28, 125
Apprenticeships, 38, 42
Asian American children:
foster care disparities, 73, 84
identity issues, 117, 120–121
model minority, 83
See also Chinese adoptees; Korean adoptees
Asian children, adoption of:
American racial preferences, 82, 127
humanitarian adoptions, 95, 102
Australian aboriginal children, 88

Baatombu people, 16–20, 30–31, 34–35
Baby farms, 39, 42
Baby selling or buying, 10, 110, 112
Baby traffickers, 44
Bartholet, Elizabeth, 81
Benin, 16–20, 30–31, 126
"Best interests of the child" priorities, 40, 43, 73, 80, 88, 90, 100
Bibliography, 132–141
Biological determinism, 51
Birth control, 51, 66, 72, 104, 109
Birth mothers:
continuing relationship with child and adoptive parents, 129
emotional reactions to giving up babies, 52–53

fitness for parenthood, 43
postwar changing attitudes, 49–50
socioeconomic class and adoption choices, 58–61
See also Single mothers
Birth parents:
adopting parent payments to, 10
natural versus adoptive parents, 27–29, 43
parental rights and children in foster care, 67
unfit parent standards, 66
Birth rates outside of marriage, 48
Birth records confidentiality, 46–48, 52
Bledsoe, Caroline, 35
Blended families, 50, 131
Blood relations and parenthood, 24–25, 27–29, 37, 43, 109
Boarding school system, for Native Americans, 87
Brace, Charles Loring, 41
Briggs, Laura, 86, 96, 126–127
Brown, Caroline, 90

Cameroon, 17, 20, 30–31
Canada, 87–88, 91, 102, 104, 108
Catholic children, 45
Child fostering cultures. See Cultural differences in child circulation
Child gender preferences, 69–71, 113–114
Child labor, 39
Child mortality rates, 38, 39
Child neglect definitions, 84–85
Child-parent matching and placement, 45, 51–52
Child protection, 38–41
Child protective services, 85
Child-raising responsibility, 30–31
individuals, community, and society, 124
women's motherhood role, 43–44
Child removal inequities, 68, 83–85, 87–88, 92–93
Children's economic role, 38–39
Children with special needs, 62, 65, 86
Chinese abandoned girls, 69–71, 103, 113–114

Chinese adoptees, 116
  adopting family characteristics, 117
  adoptive parents and cultural issues,
    120–121
  identity issues, 2, 117–118, 120–121
  family support resources, 118
Chinese adoption, 69–71, 113–116
  adoptive parent sexual orientation
    and, 115, 117
  American attitudes toward China, 115
  American racial preferences and,
    82, 127
  costs of, 57
  domestic norms, 70
  government role in, 69, 71, 113,
    114, 115
  one family's experience, 123
  sex preferences, 70–71, 114
  transnational adoption trends, 97,
    103–104, 106, 113–115
Civil Rights Act, 83
Civil rights movement, 50
Colorblindness, 74, 79, 81
Confidentiality in adoption
  documentation, 46–48, 52
Confucianism, 70, 109
Cost of adoption, 10, 57, 71, 106
Cultural connections and transnational
  families, 117–122
Cultural differences in child circulation,
  15, 93
  Andean informal fostering, 21–24,
    29, 125
  Islamic adoption issues, 24–26,
    29, 125
  natural versus adoptive parents, 27–29
  responsibility for child-raising, 30–31
  shaped by context, 31–35
  urban and rural differences, 20, 34–35
  western African social parenting,
    16–21, 30–31, 33–35

Delaney, Carol, 27–28
Demand for adoptable babies, 44–45
Displaced Persons Act, 101
Divorce rates, 50, 51, 64, 129, 131
Documentary films, 144
Doing family, 6–7, 36, 131

Doing gender, 6
Dorow, Sara, 82, 127

Eastman, P. D., 119
Ecuador, 21–24, 28
Educational issues, 34, 58, 64
Egypt, 24–26, 28
Emotional attachment, 38
Emotional reactions of birth mothers,
  52–53
Ethiopia, 95, 106, 129–130
Eugenics, 49

Families with Children from China, 118
Family counseling, 117
Family forms and norms, 2, 15
  acceptable parents for adoption or
    fostering, 63–65
  adoption and facilitating diversity,
    129–130
  adoption challenges to, 6–8
  blended families, 50, 131
  blood relations and parenthood,
    24–25, 27–29, 37, 43, 109
  child-parent matching and placement,
    45, 51–52
  Chinese gender preferences, 69–71,
    113–114
  Confucianism and, 70, 109
  contemporary Norway, 105–106
  contemporary social transformations,
    50–52
  creating "as-if begotten" families, 46
  cultural and social relatedness, 4
  doing family, 6–7, 36, 131
  keeping families together, 43
  nuclear family ideal, 5, 15, 34, 64
  postwar changing attitudes, 48–50
  public and private, 56
  responsibility for child-raising, 30–31
  social engineering, 49
  understanding diversity of, 5–6
  unfit parent standards, 66
  urban and rural differences,
    20, 34–35
  U.S. adoption controversies, 42–44
Family kinship blood bonds. See Blood
  relations and parenthood

Fanshel, David, 88
Fertility rates, 44. *See also* Infertility
Fictional literature, 145–146
Fogg-Davis, Hawley, 81
Fonseca, Claudia, 3
Formal adoption, 9
  government laws and policies, 9
  statistics on, 11–13
Fosterage cultures. *See* Cultural
  differences in child circulation
Foster care, 66–68, 86–87
  American children as damaged goods,
    96, 127
  child removal inequities, 68, 83–85,
    87–88, 92–93
  financial support, 68–69, 85
  Native Americans and, 87–88
  racial/ethnic disparities, 73, 78–79,
    83–87, 92–93, 125–126
  statistics, 66, 67, 86
France, 96

Gauthier, Mary, 3
Gay and lesbian parents, 62, 65, 66,
  115, 117
Gay liberation movement, 50
Gender and education, 34
Gender performance
  ("doing" gender), 6–7
Gender preferences, Chinese, 69–71,
  113–114
Gender roles, 50
Genetics, 51
  race and, 76
Germany, 102
Goody, Esther, 30
Government influence. *See* State
  influence
Guatemala, 97, 111–113, 126

Hague Convention on the
  Protection of Children,
  99–101, 104
Hair care, 81
Hernandez, Sarah, 89
Higginbotham, Elizabeth, 74
Higher education and adoption
  choices, 58

Historical perspectives. *See* Adoption in
  the U.S., historical perspectives
Humanitarian adoptions, 95, 101–103
Hypodescent, 75–76

Immigration and Nationality Act, 102
Immigration laws, 10, 104
India, 95
Indian Child Welfare Act (ICWA),
  73, 89–91, 100, 124
Infant adoption, 10–11, 51
  demand for adoptable babies,
    44–45
  demand for white infants,
    81–82, 103
  economic issues, 42
  transnational adoption demand
    and, 104
Infertility, 58, 105, 109
Informal adoption, 9. *See also* Cultural
  differences in child circulation;
  Foster care
Informal conjugal relationships, 31
Informal fosterage cultures. *See* Cultural
  differences in child circulation
Intercountry adoption. *See*
  Transnational adoption
International adoption. *See*
  Transnational adoption
International Korean Adoption
  Service, 118
Internet resources, 118, 142, 144
Interracial adoption. *See* Transracial
  adoption
Irish Americans, 82
Islamic adoption issues, 24–26,
  27, 29, 125

Japan, 102
Jewish people, 45
Jones, Edmund D., 80
Journal special issues, 147

Korean adoptees:
  identity issues, 1, 117, 119
  support resources, 118
Korean transnational adoption trends,
  95, 97, 102, 107–109

Latino children, foster care disparities, 73, 84
Lebanon, 24–26, 28
Leigh, Mike, 76
Leinaweaver, Jessaca, 32–33
Lindsey, Duncan, 84

Massachusetts adoption law, 39–40
Mbondossi community, 17, 20
Memoirs and remembrances, 145
Mende people, 17
Mexican Americans, 82
Military adoptions, 102
Minnesota Children's Code, 45
Motherhood role of women, 43–44
Mothers. See Birth mothers; Single mothers
Movie resources, 143–144

National Association of Black Social Workers (NABSW), 79–80, 83, 91
National Council for Adoption (NCFA), 13
Native Americans, 87–91
   adoptee adjustment issues, 88–89
   adoption and foster placement inequities, 73
   boarding schools, 87
   Indian Adoption Project, 88
   Indian Child Welfare Act, 73, 89–91, 100, 124
Natural parents versus adoptive parents, 27–29, 43
New Zealand, 102
Norway, 69, 71–72, 97, 105–106, 126
Notermans, Catrien, 31
Nuclear family, 5, 15, 34, 64

Older child adoption, 10, 11, 42
   adjustment problems, 88, 127
   economic considerations, 38–39, 41
Open adoption, 52–53, 127
Orphanages, 41–42, 103, 110, 114
Orphans:
   African war and AIDS orphans, 35, 129–130
   humanitarian adoptions, 101–102

Islam and, 25, 26
   Korean War, 107
   Orphan trains, 40–41
Ortiz, Ana, 96, 126–127

Parental loss effects, 38
Parents. See Adoptive parents; Birth parents; Family forms and norms
Peru, 23–24, 32–33
Poverty, 106
   child removal and neglect definitions, 84–85
   children and, 61–62
   explaining transnational adoption, 96, 107, 127
   single mothers and, 58–60
   See also Race and ethnicity; Socioeconomic class
Power and status differentials, 7–8, 15–16, 126
Private adoption, 10, 39, 126
Private adoption agencies, 9–10, 44, 86, 110, 112. See also Adoption agencies
Professionalization of adoption, 44
Public adoption agencies, 9–10, 49, 67, 86, 90. See also Adoption agencies

Race and ethnicity, 73
   adopted children's experiences, 80–82
   adoption and revealing social lines of division, 127
   colorblindness, 74, 79, 81
   foster placement inequities, 73, 78, 83–85
   genetic variations, 76
   hair care, 81
   hypodescent and mixed-race unions, 75–76
   informal fosterage, 125–126
   overt racism, 92
   race as a problematic category, 74–77
   racial matching policies, 46, 52, 77
   transnational adoption issues, 128
   transracial adoption issues, 79–83
   U.S. adoption history, 77–79

white privilege of adoption,
    81–83, 125
See also Transracial adoption; specific
    minorities
Racial identity, 74–75, 81, 117,
    128–129
Racial mixing, 45–46, 52
Racism, 74, 80, 83, 92, 119, 121, 129
Refugee adoption legislation, 101–102
Refugee Relief Act of 1953, 102
Regulation. See Adoption law and
    regulation; State influence
Religion and adoption, 24–26, 45
Reproductive technologies, 106
Rieger, Lisa, 90
Riley, Nancy E., 148
Roberts, Dorothy, 83–85, 88, 91
Romania, 103, 109–111, 127
Roorda, Rhona, 128
Rothman, Barbara Katz, 4, 6, 77, 79, 81
Russian Federation, 97

Same-sex marriages, 62, 66
Secrecy in adoption records, 46–48, 52
Secrets and Lies, 76, 79, 144
Sexual orientation, 62–63, 65,
    66, 115, 117
Sexual revolution, 50–51
Shining Path (Sendero Luminoso),
    32–33
Sierra Leone, 17, 35
Simon, Rita, 89, 128
Single men as parents, 62, 65
Single mothers:
    banned from public education, 64
    fitness for parenthood, 43, 51, 64–65
    postwar normalization of, 50
    socioeconomic class and adoption
        choices, 58–60
    stigma, 43, 48, 51, 65, 126
    See also Birth mothers
Single-parent families, 64
Skin color matching, 46
Social engineering, 49
Social parenthood practices of west
    Africa, 16–21, 30–31, 33–35, 93
Social welfare policies, 68–69, 86
Social workers, 41

"best interests of the child" priorities, 43
child placement efforts, 45
NABSW statement against transracial
    adoption, 79–80, 83, 91
Socioeconomic class, 57–60
    child removal and neglect definitions,
        84–85
    complex social issues, 129
    government intervention and, 66–67
    hypodescent and mixed-race unions,
        75–76
    power gradients and child transfer,
        7–8
    See also Poverty
Sociological perspectives, 4, 125, 126–127
Solinger, Rickie, 2
South Korean transnational adoption
    trends, 95, 97, 102, 107–109
Special needs children, 62, 65, 86
Sperm donation, 71, 106
Spivak, Gayatri, 74
Stack, Carol, 78
State influence, 5, 32, 44–45, 56, 65–69, 92
    child removal inequities, 68, 83–85,
        87–88, 92–93
    China and, 69–71
    formal adoption laws and policies, 9
    Norway and, 71–72
    subsidies, 68–69, 71, 85–86, 106
    See also Adoption law and regulation;
        Foster care
Stranger adoption, 9, 61, 105
Strong, Pauline Turner, 74
Strong adoption, 9
Subsidies, 68–69, 85–86
Substitute care arrangements, 38
Sudan, 26
Sullk'ata, 21, 28
Support groups, 118

Tax credits, 86
Transnational adoption, 10, 52, 94
    ambiguity and complex issues, 129–130
    continuing home country contact, 95
    costs, 106
    family counseling, 117
    Hague Convention and, 99–101, 104
    humanitarian, 95, 101–103

immigration laws and, 10
interracial adoption issues, 82, 115,
    116, 121, 128
making families and cultural
    connections, 116–122
one parent's hopes and worries, 123
savable children, 96, 127
sending and receiving country
    statistics, 96–99
sending country issues, 95, 105–106,
    107–116
statistics on, 12
terminology, 94
undesirability of poor American
    children, 96, 127
U.S. and, 96, 104–105
See also Cultural differences in child
    circulation
Transracial adoption, 79–83, 128–129
    adopted children's experiences,
        80–82, 88–89
    as white privilege, 81–83
    NABSW statement against, 79–80,
        83, 91
    Native Americans and, 87–91
    transnational adoption issues,
        82, 116, 121
    See also Race and ethnicity
Turkey, 27

Ukraine, 97
UN Convention on the
    Rights of the Child, 33, 91
Unfit parent standards, 66
Urban and rural differences in child
    fosterage, 20, 34–35

Vance, Carol, 26
Van Vleet, Krista E., 148
Van Winkle, Barrik, 74
Visibility of adoptive families,
    2, 8, 14, 56, 131

War effects on child circulation,
    32–33, 35
War orphans, 35, 102, 107
Wawachakuy, 21–24
Websites, 118, 142, 144
Weismantel, Mary, 27–29
Western African child fostering
    practices, 16–21, 30–31,
    33–35, 93
Whiteness norms, 79
White privilege of adoption,
    81–83, 125
Williams, Patricia, 80
Women's movement, 50

Zelizer, Viviana, 53

About the Authors

Krista E. Van Vleet is an anthropology professor at Bowdoin College. Her research focuses on the practices and politics of kinship and gender in the Andes. She is particularly interested in how native Andeans produce relatedness in their everyday interactions and in contexts shaped by the transnational movements of people, images, ideas, and commodities. Her first book, *Performing Kinship: Narrative, Gender, and the Intimacies of Power in the Andes* (2008, University of Texas Press) intertwines folk stories, personal narratives, and interviews with detailed descriptions of people's social relationships in a rural Bolivian community. Her more recent research explores discourses of family, gender, and morality among Andean Catholics, international missionaries, and evangelical Protestants in Cusco, Peru. She is also currently engaged in research on the interrelationships of narrative and nonverbal expression and is exploring the use of digital video in research and teaching.

Nancy E. Riley is a sociology professor at Bowdoin College. Her research focuses on family, gender, and population and China. She is interested in how the recent changes in China have affected women's lives in families. She has recently finished a monograph, *Laboring in Paradise: Gender, Work, and Family in a Chinese Economic Zone,* based on her research in Dalian on the family lives of married women factory workers. Her current projects include an edited volume exploring the connections between gender and demographic changes and a new project on domestic adoption within China.